Psychology Revivals

Archetypes

Man is dominated by his archetypes; they mould not only his history but his dreams. But how are we to define and evaluate them? Is it perhaps possible for us to relate more creatively to them?

Originally published in 1981, these are some of the questions raised by this title. To answer them the author gathered together a vast amount of material drawn from Eastern and Western traditions, from science, literature, art and poetry. The answers he puts forward are often highly original and will surely challenge many of our most cherished patterns of thought.

There emerges from this book what can only be described as a global metaphysical system, yet the author's language is not that of an ordinary metaphysical treatise, and what he writes offered new challenge and hope to those suffering from the despair and cynicism engendered by a great deal in modern society at the time. Zolla does not, however, advocate a return to earlier historical patterns, nor is he proposing a new Utopia, but rather offers us a brilliant series of lessons in the art of centring. In the words of Bernard Wall, writing in the *Times Literary Supplement*, Zolla's 'deep, polymathic probing of the terms of human existence makes it sensible to compare him with Simone Weil, while some of his conclusions about ultimate mysteries – expressed in signs, symbols and sacraments, the sense of which we have lost – will make us think of the later T. S. Eliot'.

Archetypes

Elémire Zolla

Routledge
Taylor & Francis Group
LONDON AND NEW YORK

First published in 1981
by George Allen & Unwin Ltd

This edition first published in 2015 by Routledge
27 Church Road, Hove BN3 2FA

and by Routledge
711 Third Avenue, New York, NY 10017

Routledge is an imprint of the Taylor & Francis Group, an informa business

Publisher's Note
The publisher has gone to great lengths to ensure the quality of this reprint but points out that some imperfections in the original copies may be apparent.

Disclaimer
The publisher has made every effort to trace copyright holders and welcomes correspondence from those they have been unable to contact.

ISBN: 978-1-138-92102-3 (hbk)
ISBN: 978-1-315-68663-9 (ebk)
ISBN: 978-1-138-92108-5 (pbk)

ARCHETYPES

by

ELEMIRE ZOLLA

London
GEORGE ALLEN & UNWIN
Boston Sydney

First published in 1981

GEORGE ALLEN & UNWIN LTD
40 Museum Street, London WC1A 1LU

British Library Cataloguing in Publication Data

Zolla, Elemire
Archetypes.
1. Metaphysics
I. Title
110 BD111 80-41389

ISBN 0-04-111007-2

Set in 11 on 13 point Plantin by Bedford Typesetters Ltd
and printed in Great Britain
by Lowe & Brydone Limited,
Thetford, Norfolk

Contents

IV

Archetypal poetry

V

The Vision of the Rose

I *Metaphysical Experience*

1 Metaphysical experience

When the experiencing psyche and the things it perceives, subject and object, melt and are absorbed into one another, what takes place may be called 'metaphysical experience'. I think this is a good designation, but it should be periodically checked, and replaced before it sounds hollow and shrill, before it is taken for granted. In Sanskrit it would be *asamprajñasamâdhi*. Sanskrit is the best tool for dealing with the topic. It has been pointed out that it lavishes twenty accurate, nicely defined different terms on what Western languages brutishly lump together as 'consciousness'.

The compound *asamprajñasamâdhi* is made up of a string of words, each of them adding a touch to the global meaning.

Samâdhi is the gathering in of the mind, which becomes detached from all that the roving eye, the eager ear, the savouring tongue, the thrilled skin and, deeper still, untiring recollection and wild imagination assail it with, like a tortoise tucking in head, tail and feet, turning inward, away from what may be battering at its shell. The aloof mind concentrates on its self-colouredness, becomes absorbed in its self-existent identity and sameness. Same and *samâdhi* stem from the same root.

In *samâdhi* the compacted, unified self can say 'I am', but no longer 'I am this or that'.

This is not a deprivation. The words used so far: 'gathering in', 'tucking in', 'detachment' and 'absorption', should convey not a depletion but an unshackling, an enrichment, a mounting elation.

'I am' is prior to, more vast than 'I am this' or 'I am that'. It denotes being uncoerced, potential, uncommitted, not confined by verbalisation. The demarcation between selfhood and being is ignored, and disappears. Sensations are there as always, but now the mind is all there as never before, unimpressed by them, not attending to them, allowing them to rise and vanish unspoilt by its own exertions and judgements, undisturbed by all involvement and worry, left to the freshness of their origination, unsullied by mental chatter and commentary. They are no longer felt as something alien, external, so the mind is literally all. It may apparently be occupied in tackling events, and it even does so with unique lucidity and promptness, but remaining untouched, unfragmented, fully unidentified with results. It has forgotten what it is to fuss.

Samâdhi is hard to describe because nothing of it need transpire externally. It lacks identification marks. As an inward reality, on the other hand, it is a total attitude that defies all violent, oppositional binary formulations.

It is the self-awareness of the self, but also absolute impersonality.

It is *I am*, but it is equally *what is*.

In *samâdhi* the psyche may be totally caught in the ecstatic realisation of unity, of its own unity as well as of the unity of itself and the world, but it may also, apart from this, smoothly, systematically identify with the flow of events. These are now seen by it as manifestations of being, of universal, all-embracing, sheer being which is the *samâdhi*-self. The *samâdhi*-self is an unjudging self, which no longer bothers to distinguish good and evil and the other dyads, but detects the oneness of everything. Dwelling at 'the still point of the turning world', it is aware as it needs to be of events without having to focus on them. In its ease and openness it lets them flow into itself; it is an unopposing sea, a clear, shining mirror.

The reverse of *samâdhi* is what old-fashioned psychiatry termed 'neurasthenia', a deliberate dwelling on events, a clinging to sensations, a grappling with them, a harking back on them. With neurasthenia every perception is sifted, every wayward image indulged in, dragged into self-conscious focus. The glutted mind staggers, and falls to daydreaming. The neurasthenic's paradox is that he is both stuck in the irrelevance of the merely factual and lost in the blur of fancy. What is hell on earth but this pointless, relentless retailing of existence utterly unrelieved by meditation, totally unacquainted with collectedness, lacking any hint of *samâdhi*? With supreme pity and horror Tolstoy depicted neurasthenia in its terminal exasperation, describing the last, haggard, drugged days of Anna Karenina. Joyce took pleasure in recording its gluey psychic fermentations, as though for him nothing else truly existed. The stream of consciousness is the river of hell. Neurasthenia is consequent on a total exposure and vulnerability to sensations and fancy; it fetters the mind and the psyche to the irredeemable, tormented multiplicity of an alien world. *Samâdhi* instead skims reality, which it does not feel distinct from itself; it leisurely, unconcernedly, obliviously takes in and breathes out the world. Naval officers are trained in *samâdhi* when taught to look out for submarines by resting their gaze on the far horizon, not fixing on any one section of the sea; monks receive instruction in the art of never going back over events, of avoiding complacency and self-consciousness by soaring above the flow of reality and discarding the flutter of day-dreams. There is a delightful recipe for *samâdhi* among Karmapa Tibetan monks; when you feel dull, meditate on an imaginary white bean in the midst of your brow; when agitated, imagine a black bean at the bottom of your spine and concentrate on that; when dull and agitated ('grey'), the bean shall be azure and must be placed in front of you at your shadow's end. Jack of the Beanstalk made a bargain when he exchanged all he had for a few coloured beans.

When the monkey neurasthenia which most men carry on their shoulders has dissolved into thin air, there is no need to play about with beans any longer. One may now, as Marianne Moore put it:

flee
to metaphysical newmown hay,
honeysuckle or wood's fragrance.

When neurasthenic self-adjustments and scrutinies cease, awareness becomes unusually, even preternaturally keen. St Theresa fried eggs during her ecstasies. She pulled the pan off the fire in the nick of time.

Vedânta speaks of mind placing itself beyond the duality of the conscious and the unconscious, of waking and sleeping. Greek *anastenarides* fire-walkers baffle observers by being entranced and alert at the same time. It is precisely when uncontrived and ego-less that minds grasp truths in a flash. *Samâdhi* is unification and quietude, the contrary of torpor, even if it might sometimes look like coma. Stupor and the swoon of an in-gathering mind are worlds apart, but people conditioned to appreciate tense, deliberate, cramped modes of life tend to mistake one for the other.

The inwardness and surrender of *samâdhi* are the conditions of rapid realisations, of lucky, dashing interventions; the accurate hit and guess and the ultimate, finishing stroke are its privilege. A paradigm of *samâdhi* is the Japanese art of archery, which consists in taking one's mind off the arrow and becoming the bull's eye. Through utter amalgamation, *samâdhi* realises the essences of things and events, by feeling itself at their root, as their creator. It is a selfless self-absorption into a selfhood which is being as such, in itself.

One may live with a man in *samâdhi* and never be aware of it. His spirited tackling of events can be mistaken for active participation and concern, his aloofness for torpor.

But at concerts we have a chance to isolate and pinpoint *samâdhi*.

The moment the performance ends, the ensuing silence is filled with the substance of the music, teems with its meanings. The overtones which spilled and rippled out of the concluding note have now faded away; for a split second there are no more sounds; only their significance is left. The concert is over, but still the applause dares not follow. After and beyond the last quiver, the essence, the thrill lingers on. The composition stands out condensed, epitomised before us, within us, as it loomed compact and germinal before the composer, within him, the instant his hand rushed to jot it down.

The progressive build-up of the execution is at its inaudible climax, it has reached its silent sabbath, and in the void the music's activating essence, its very being, is set free. This *is* what was slowly unfurled in the course of the winding hesitations and streams of melody. For a rapt instant the whole composition is inaudibly, pre-acoustically present. The listener is one not so much with the music, which is played out, as with its inmost being, which made it possible, impelled it into existence: with *how* rather than with *what* it is.

The burst of applause that now follows is the avowal of the intolerable bliss of the listener's utter fusion with the music, subject with object.

The very same fusion takes place not only at the finale but relatively, proportionally, at every pause. Shelley's Ione suggests:

> Listen too,
> How every pause is filled with under-notes,
> Clear, silver, icy, keen, awakening tones,
> Which pierce the sense, and live within the soul.

The knower and the known, oneself and being itself, become one and the same in *samprajñasamâdhi*: the *samâdhi* of the knowledge (*prajñâ*) of the sameness (*sam-*) of the knower and the known; of ultimate selfhood, identity as such on the one hand and being as such on the other.

When the three – the actual, known being, the godlike knower, and the beauty, the bliss of knowing – combine and become one, all remembrance of a particular, limited, personal selfhood vanishes, so the negative particle *a-* is prefixed and the compound *asamprajñasamâdhi* results. Its pathetic illustration is the enthralled listener, hands irresistibly clapping, eyes curtained by tears, beyond himself, above all remembrance of himself.

2 Loss of face

Metaphysical experience, then, connotes an experience transcending the person, who may later recall it as having apparently taken place somehow in relation with him or her; it consists of an awareness of being on the brink of manifestation, in its germinative unity, a unity which is the triad of knower, known and knowing clasped together. It may be described as being in a pre-incarnate, higher condition, in which limitations and delusions – names and shapes – are ignored. Feelings and thoughts are, at this level, on an infinite, unlimited scale, uncompromised with minor, inessential concerns. The mind is mere flowing music, its song is one with the hidden melody of the surrounding world: what the true musician uncovers, without adding one note of his own. Music identifies *how* things are rather than *what* they are; it captures the quality that makes events what they are rather than their circumscribed appearance, which, separated from its quality, is nothing but a fictitious name tagged on to a delusive shape.

Real life is the triad of knower, known and knowing, uncircumscribed by a name or a shape: the sheer song of the world. From here man falls into the everyday delusion of names and shapes, 'opens his eyes', as the Serpent suggests, splitting the flow of being into opposing names and shapes, through the 'knowledge of good and evil'.

Metaphysical experience consists precisely in not consenting to the fall, in staying poised as far as possible above, within the music.

Of course the fall takes place, but it can be ignored more than is usually believed. A name and a shape are forced on everyone entering the world of names and shapes, but if the inner ear still harks to the secret melody, which is nothing but the music of the flow of the world, one remains inwardly free – whatever masks are assumed. One is not the social selves one may take on. One is faceless; beneath one's mask there is only music, a resonant void.

Blunted, worldly minds forget about all this and their social mask becomes the flesh of their face. So they become terrified at the thought that it might be wrenched off them, at the possibility of a loss of face. When one has attained to metaphysical experience, one's face is only the mask one happened to pick up casually at the threshold of the fallen world – where one practices, or rather lets one's shape practice the delusions of name and shape, but without ever forgetting that all is deceit.

The shape and name one happens to assume in the fallen world, viewed from the musical nowness in which one truly lives, are nothing but a speck in infinite space, no more necessarily 'one's own' than any other shape and name – than any other face. Good riddance!

At moments of extreme intensity even in ordinary life there is a craving to shed one's own person. Even in common love affairs people sometimes behave madly and wickedly because they feel too intensely to stand the trammels of selfhood. A character in *Nightwood*, caught in such a mood, mutters about her lover: 'I will do something that she will never be able to forgive, then we can begin again as strangers.'

Once faceless, stripped of one's person, one ceases to revere the fact of having been born of certain parents in a certain place. At this point, one proclaims with a flourish: 'The Sun is my Father and the Moon is my Mother' or 'I was born of Father Sky and Mother Earth.' One's personal history is cast off as a wearisome burden. There is a Polish play in which each actor carries a limp puppet. An actress starts dancing to a grotesque little waltz, and the puppets begin to move. Soon it is they that seem to be carrying the actors, as men are carried along by their biographies.

3 The face one had before being born

With the first gust of liberation the puppet is dropped; one disidentifies with one's biography. Life stories are seen through. They are dreams, jokes, games, all the more so when they tell the legends of our grosser, madder selves – the legends of our tribe, or planet. Politicians treat these things for what they are, moulding them like lumps of clay to suit the need of the moment.

A history of the world is a toy for power-obsessed, abstract-minded adults, who find no rest until history, which is a chimera, is fancied into something amenable to their pompous games – either a poem full of ups and downs written by somebody very much like themselves or a mechanical contraption of dented cogwheels. They will squeeze the 'world' up through the tunnel of progressive evolution, or twist it round and round to fit revolving cycles, or dash it into an upshooting spiral or finally thrust it down a maelstrom.

One grows bored with all this, and finally quietly dismisses it out of mere intellectual honesty.

From a higher point of view, a Vedantic master (Nisargadhatta Maharaj) observed: 'Why should I invent patterns for creation, evolution and destruction? The world is in me. I am not afraid of it and have no desire to lock it up in a mental picture.'

The statement implies that what we experience depends on how we conceive. We cannot avoid conceiving, but we are free to conceive as we will and what we will. Very few make bold to assert their freedom of conception. Most people are conceited, but they make do with paltry and silly representations of themselves. Delusions of grandeur are mistakes not in themselves but because with such energy one might conceive on so much grander a scale. Vedânta suggests that we feel the world in us and not vice versa; that we identify with timeless, spaceless infinity. Infinity is something which we project on the outside world, and which we alienate from ourselves. Once alienated, infinity becomes a contradiction in terms, a finite quantity: at the most we may reach 10^{10} light-years, 10^{28} cm in the outgoing direction, and 10^{-14} cm in the inward-moving direction; the intervening gap of 10^{42} cm is all the infinity that computers can stretch out of figures. True infinity is reeled up inside the mind. It is in the one who conceives it, so identification with infinity is the acknowledgement of a fact.

'I am infinite' is simple truth and by acknowledging it one is simply being sensible. One stands the chance of making an infinite gain if one succeeds in realising it as a living experience. The Mass seeks to convey in a pantomime that, since man is by nature a claimant, he might as well lay claim to Allness, and that the way to do so is to eat, incorporate, become self-sufficing, self-eating Allness. To avoid inflating the ego, Jung pointed out, the process was assumed not to be willed and performed by man, who only ministered to the pantomime of powerful similes, of son-torturing fathers, cannibal siblings and Self-eating Selves.

The I that succeeds in becoming the universe overcomes man's central, abstract terror, the root of dread in his heart, which is the sense of separation and isolation from the world, and hence of a surrounding cosmic, indistinct hostility. Cosmic dread shows the need for self-identification with the world. The usual diagnosis – lack of love – is formally correct, but sounds hopelessly sentimental since the idea of the fusion of the microcosm with the macrocosm is lacking.

Grand, universal-minded arch-swindlers thrive and wax

powerful on primal, latent, ever-lurking dread, for which they provide an 'explanation of the universe' that locks up the world, the dreaded Thing, in a mental prison. They offer to quell thereby what Vedânta teaches us to uproot. The uprooting is done by identifying with the source of terror: the All, Timelessness, Spacelessness.

The bold art of conceiving the universe as one's (true) self should be taught after the learner has accepted the basic Vedantic idea, which only Shakespeare and Calderón have divulged in the West, that waking and dreaming are equal. They are the refutation of one another. Once it is inwardly realised that in dreams history is no more real than dreams are in history, the constructs of the waking mind can be disposed of with the same ease with which dreams are dropped at sunrise.

Society-worshippers object to the granting of reality-status to dreams on the ground that they are merely private affairs. This is beside the point, and the assertion itself is not correct. In societies in which dreams are keenly attended to, they are considered the highest form of social intercourse. Joseph received intelligence of Mary's condition by dreaming of the same angel who made the announcement to her. In serious initiations it is indispensable that the candidate share dreams with the initiator. Two instances, chosen at random: the consecration to Isis narrated in *The Golden Ass*, preceded by a dream visit of the goddess intimating the same message, both to the supplicant and to her priest; and the Hako ceremony of the Plains Indians, in which a company of worshippers of the goddess concentrate ritually on a man in some distant camp, whom they wish to initiate. They send the goddess to visit him in his dreams and next dispatch a party of scouts to pitch their tents on the border of his camp, where he will join them, having been forewarned of their arrival in his dreams.

But this is relatively simple. In order to attain to metaphysical experience, waking should be the equal not only of dreaming, but also of sleeping. A Vedantic master (T. M. P. Mahadevan) suggests meditating on the phrase 'I have happily slept', especially on the 'I' which it involves. It is an experience of I-ness that one should be able to recapture by abstracting from both the waking and the dreaming I. The accent of the phrase can be on the 'I': '*I* have happily slept.' There is wonder at being the selfsame I. The pretence of some sort of continuity between the present and the sleeping I is actually rather quaint. But on the verge of awakening or of falling asleep, poised above wakefulness and dreaming, there persists a trace of the sleeping I – the lingering on or the anticipation of an undetermined, infinite, unified, universal I blissfully above all identification with a 'this' or a 'that', but not totally beyond a 'thus', since one can say 'I *happily* slept' or 'shall *happily* sleep'. As the quietude of the slumbering I draws close, metaphysical experience is approached.

It may be objected that there exists no direct experience of the sleeping I, since there are no means of checking whether it is actually remembered or only imagined. The same has been maintained of the dreaming I, on the ground that all we possess are the apparent reminiscences of dreams, not the dreams themselves. But the argument can be extended also against the waking I, because its seemingly direct experiences are essentially recollections.

Actually sleep can certainly be a direct experience, because it interpenetrates waking. It is the inadvertences, the discontinuity of wakefulness. Waking is like a flashing of discrete quanta of awareness, and the intervals in between, the lapses in wakefulness, are of the substance of sleep. Just as in concerts the silent climax is of the same substance as the myriad pauses within the texture of the music, so sleep is nothing but the climax of the essential discontinuity of wakefulness.

The *Imitation of Christ* proposes as a theme of meditation the query: Where are you when you are not mentally present? But one is automatically efficient, and lucid beyond attentiveness during peak performances, when self-awareness ceases. When most awake one is asleep.

One sometimes happily gasps: 'I have lost all sense of time and space' – a commonplace with lovers, fighters, artists, and with anybody deeply engaged in so absorbing a task that he is as in deep sleep.

Once one realises that, when most involved, one is fast asleep, one perceives clearly the subtle I of 'I *have* happily slept', a marginal, elusive, quick I, the I of rapturous sleep-walking, or simply of all the moments in life in which one glides along one's predestined path. In a night's sleep, wondrous feats are accomplished. Loads and loads of inanity are happily dumped into nothingness. Immense strides towards liberation are happily taken in the depths of sleep. It would be enough if at the magical transition of awakening, one could hold on to the sensation of having happily slept; then during the day one would be perfection perfected.

And yet there is an ingrained resistance to the conclusion that the sleeping I is the ideal I-ness. This depends on the latent assumption that consciousness is superior to being, a prejudice that ignores the possibility of their ultimate fusion and does not consider that eventually the primacy of being might be more reasonably asserted.

Once the sleeping I is realised, one can even answer that Zen challenge: 'Show me the face you had before you were born.'

4 Ins and outs, alchemical transformations

The I of metaphysical experience is identity as such, the principle of unification itself. It is oneness, which precedes all births into multiplicity. Something less or more than what persists of the I in deep sleep is preserved in metaphysical experience – which may appear as something less than the waking I, but also as much more than that. It is the blending of all the many waking selves, as Vedânta calls them: the seeing, the hearing, the smelling self, and with them the reminiscing, the imagining self, fused in an unruffled, indistinct, all-embracing I-ness. In describing it, it matters little whether the similes of inwardness or of outwardness are used. It is unity, which can either be an in-gathering or an outgoing blending with a landscape, a soul, a rhythm, an odour, with whatever; and in the blending that in which one blends becomes Allness.

At the utmost pitch of intensity, when perception becomes, to use Keats's compound, swooning-vivid, it blends the perceiver and the perceived. It is equally true that it is a restriction and that it is an expansion – a blotting out of the outer world and an identification with it. The two contrary similes are interchangeable.

The concentrated meditator, his eyes closed, drawn into the inner maelstrom of nothingness which is allness, is equivalent to the worshipper of nature staring enrapt, winging through the landscape, swallowed up in vastness, in an allness which is nothingness. In either case identification with one's everyday, ever-moving, restless psyche and mind ceases. As the disidentification becomes sharper, it matters less and less whether the psyche feels what is taking place as a leaning to leeward or to windward, whether objects (the word means: projections) are conceived as inside or outside our skin, whether we are dealing with recollections on their way out, into oblivion, or on their way in, at their inception. No perception can be wrenched out of the mental categories that frame it, and no category can be stripped from its object; convex and concave cannot be sliced off a dome.

Samâdhi (meditation) is metaphysical experience (*asamprajñasamâdhi*) still unachieved, still intent on overcoming distracting thoughts and images; worship of nature is metaphysical experience with a surviving sense of separateness from nature. There is no difference between getting lost in inner or in outer space, since as Wordsworth explained, the two are one:

> In many a walk
> At evenings or by moonlight, or reclined
> At midday upon beds of forest moss
> Have we to Nature and her impulses
> Of our whole being made free gift and when
> Our trance had left us, oft have we, by aid
> Of the impressions which it left behind,
> Looked inward at our selves, and learned, perhaps
> Something of what we are.

When one's whole being melts into music, where is the fusion taking place? In the vibrations or in the innermost self? On the convex or in the concave of the ear's inmost coil? Call this fusion a diving in, or a rushing forth of selfhood, it is its own unification beyond the dyad, beyond in and out. The psyche may reflect it as a wave of bliss or as a serene quietude, as a laborious achievement or a soothing gift: in itself it is mere, naked presence.

Whose presence, presence to what? These questions now mean little. A subject nakedly present is not a separate entity clinging to his separateness: he or she has become everybody and nobody. As for the presence itself, it confronts an Ineffable Person – who is the living wholeness or perfection of being; whose art, or creativeness, is nature; whose body is the universe. Strict Vedânta considers the stage in which one uses these terms below the one in which the Ineffable is expressed by the neuter singular, *Brahman*, and not by the masculine singular, *Brahmâ*. Of course the path of passionate, loving devotion needs the living person of the Godhead, but even here there comes the stage in which there is no longer a lover and a beloved, but only love.

Whenever the psyche is at peace, metaphysical experience cannot be far away. When particular emotions, reasonings, imaginations, identifications fall from one's shoulders, the goal is at hand.

All are bound to have made contact with it to some extent, in passing, because no psychic or intellectual life can subsist without some balance of its elements, without some measure, however temporary and unstable, of quietude. Metaphysical experience is indeed nearer man than his jugular vein. It is comparable to air: an ancient simile, which the Cabbalists and Petrarch pursued into the smallest detail. Metaphysical experience sustains all life within man, as air nourishes all earthly creatures. The experience of oneness, the only non-contradictory reality, is reflected in the mind as the first law of reason, the principle of non-contradiction, and in the psyche as quietude.

Air is all around, but it is elusiveness itself; everybody is immersed in metaphysical experience, but few can grasp it. As it needs the training of an athlete to breathe properly, or rather to be properly, powerfully breathed by air, so spiritual warfare must be waged if metaphysical experience is to become the pivot of life, or, rather, if life is to become its manifestation.

Everybody knows metaphysical experience at least twice a day, on awakening and on falling asleep, but only by laboriously building, at the cost of literally everything, a foothold above, in between the three states of waking, dreaming and sleeping, can that supreme experience be held on to, extended, deepened, fully enjoyed.

A neat definition of metaphysical experience is: a dreamless sleep blissfully aware of itself. Ecstatic marching as opposed to mere sleep-walking provides a vivid illustration of this point: the ecstatic marcher's radiant eyes and rapt gaze contrast graphically with the glassy, apathetic expression of the sleep-walker.

Metaphysical experience is that of the 'happy hours' Wordsworth speaks of in *This is the Spot:*

> Come, let me see thee sink into a dream
> Of quiet thoughts, protracted till thine eye
> Be calm as water when the winds are gone
> And no one can tell whither. My sweet friend,
> We two have had such happy hours together
> That my heart melts in me to think of it.

Most spiritual methods insist on a total relaxation of the body, and on the attainment of the consequent slow, deep breathing of sleep. The mind following certain methods, is first one-pointedly fixed on the breathing, and then on the heartbeat, till finally it lets go of this last hold, hovers above the slumbering body and soul as a sheer, liberated, unidentified awareness. 'Hovering above' is, literally, ecstasy.

Schelling started his classes crying: 'Gentlemen, look at that wall!' And, after a pause: 'Gentlemen, look at yourselves looking at the wall!' Perhaps few of his listeners were actually shocked into hovering above themselves. It is probable instead that quite a few of Ramana Maharshi's listeners became like disembodied witnesses when, following his instructions, they surprised themselves at prayer with the question: Who is praying?

Once the spirit is detached, the immediate result may not be peacefulness. The witnessing spirit, through its mere presence, acts like a king, and an unbalanced soul fears the presence more than death.

It will reply with an evil, sour, vacant stare; it will rise and writhe against that unbearable aloofness.

In ancient times this was compared with what happens when a plant's juice or its steeped grains are brewed through the successive transmutations of 'green alchemy'.

The body of a plant is the pulp, its soul is its essential oils, which lend it its taste and odour. When yeast, which conceals the spirit of light, starts to froth, the juices ferment. They eject their scum and foam until a new, clear, intoxicating spirit is born.

The spiritual, elevating yeast in man operates on his body and soul by simply, chasteningly repeating: 'I am not this body nor this soul. These moods, images, thoughts are external to me. I own them, they are not I' – a mere, incessant, unbearable statement of truth.

When the soul's scum and foam are ejected, thanks to unbearable truth, body and soul are transformed into a clear, intoxicating spirit.

But metaphysical experience is subject to no law. There are cases in which the souring and the boiling, the seething and the cleansing are dispensed with, as in the miracle of water turned into wine: the simple separation of the spirit from body and soul takes place in a sedate and lucid ecstasy of discovery, such as Tennyson relates in *The Ancient Sage:*

> For more than once when I myself
> Sat all alone, revolving in myself
> The word that is the symbol of myself,
> The mortal limit of the Self was loosed,
> And passed into the Nameless, as a cloud
> Melts into Heaven. I touched my limbs, the limbs
> Were strange, not mine – and yet no shade of doubt
> But utter clearness, and thro' loss of self
> The gain of such large life as match'd with ours
> Were Sun to shark – unshadowable in words.

5 Duality and time overcome

All this has been amusingly expressed and measured in terms of wavelengths. The average waking mind fires beta-waves. They correspond, in ancient parlance, to the element of earth – to purposive activity among sharply defined shapes and concepts, etched in black and white, good and bad. Everything wears a tag, is either justified or condemned. Everyday goals are taken for granted. Words firmly stand for things, each of which has a name. Time is a line running from past to future, moving with the hands of clocks, with the sun's progress in the sky.

When the body relaxes and the mind becomes less assertive, more detached, alpha-waves start flashing.

The minute hand of the clock seems to slow down. The dominant element is now that of water, of fluidity – the mode appreciative, less grasping. Objects start revealing their texture and colour; they are no longer four-square blocks, but vary with light, with the quality of the attention they receive. Situations have a flavour, suggest a feeling, an atmosphere; they are no longer cut off from the psyche, which insinuates itself into them, interpenetrates, interprets them, at the same time unfocusing immediate goals. Scenes are valued for their finer, unusual, unsettling traits, with the calm, caressing, disinterested eye of the painter. Words no longer appear soldered to things; in fact curiosity grows for their autonomous life, for their origins, their shifting, elusive qualities. The apparent clash of opposites is no longer taken for the whole story; hidden affinities are noticed behind confrontations, beneath embattled good and evil.

One becomes inured to the hard truth that reality is a function of dreams, that things are perceived according to what they symbolise, which is what caused them to be selected in the first place from myriads of others, all competing for attention. Symbolism is the language of dreams.

Having a slower time at its disposal, the Witness, the spirit, may now emerge, as distinct from the fleeting dispositions of the soul, possessed in turn by this or that archetypal dream. At this point, the puppet nature of men is realised and even the puppeteers are discerned, the master dreams that pull the strings.

Looking back at one's grasping, deliberate, dense, deluded beta-self, one realises that it is nothing more than a machine. One recognises its comicalness. The beta-self that takes pride in its matter-of-factness actually strives for the social symbols of pleasure and of status, rather than for factual happiness; it seeks money rather than what should be bought with it, packaging rather than content. In its droll world, property ends by owning its owner, who not only lives for it but cannot stand the idea of leaving it derelict, and begets heirs to keep it company. If works of art were sought for actual enjoyment there could exist no fraud, because the buyer would simply pay for the pleasure of which he would be the sole and only judge at the moment of the purchase. The possibility of forgeries and confidence tricks bears witness against the world that condemns them, in which the token is sought and not the fruition.

But this is true not only of the market-place, though here it shows at its most ludicrous. Meditation discovers that all material objects that attract and bind are nothing but keepsakes of dreams.

The meditations of the alpha-self are a prelude, the first part of a journey into the world where dreams form.

Driving deeply into reality – into oneself – after the level of earth and water, that of air is reached, theta-waves flash, the second hand of the clock moves by hops and leaps, and there are moments when it even stands still. Ecstasy sets in, as meaningfulness beyond meanings is touched – reality beyond shapes and names, which is the source of shapes and names, images and words.

Shamanism may develop at this stage, in which one learns to shuttle from one wavelength to another, becoming possessed at will by a variety of names and shapes, without forgoing the negative capability of the witnessing spirit. Lucidity and possession combine; trances are entered and dismissed as one's spiritual calling – as healer, judge, tamer, leader, diviner, poet – requires. But also the sheer, mystical repose in ecstasy is possible, when beyond names and shapes the all-encompassing silence and void is reached; the outer blends with the inner world and events become responses. At this point time stops. A man's normal self is his peculiar sense of time. And yet time is not everything, though it comprises space. A spaceship faster than light would roll time back. When theta-waves, and all the more so when delta-waves are flashed, the second hand of the clock stands perfectly still. Metaphysical experience at its peak takes place between the ticks of the clock, in the gap between heartbeats. Indeed, if time is the measure of movement, then when everything is at a standstill within there is no more time. Equally, if time is consciousness of the flow of ideas, then as the number of ideas increases, eternity is approached. Children first notice rhythm and energy of movement and only subsequently time, the inessential latecomer.

In deep meditation conflicts cease, become meaningless, and time is the joust of the two opposites – past and future. In metaphysical experience they melt into nowness, which is the climax of all time-bound endeavour, the solving of all time-caused problems, the flash of true knowledge, in which the knower and the known, past and future, coalesce in the knowing. The blending is the explanation.

A sharp separation of past and future has not always been taken for granted. In early Germanic languages yesterday and tomorrow are not distinct – the only difference in Indo-European was probably between the distant and the actually present (the suffix *-i* denoted both the present tense of verbs and the locative case of nouns). There must have been a time in which an easy-flowing awareness prevailed, not racked between harking back and worrying ahead. Here and now is the abode of love; people and things are loved only in the present tense, with no place left for prospect or retrospect. Centering makes events brim with significance, so that whatever happens now is linked to everything else taking place here and now: landscapes answer to inner moods, events are signs, feelings responses, fatality is spelt out by every event – nothing is any longer due to chance; all is destiny, meaningful coincidence. Schizophrenia sometimes offers a parody of this One-world ecstasy.

When this monadic, here-and-now, cosmos-mirroring state is approached, it is realised that space is what Hobbes, in a most metaphysical vein, defined: nothing but what we project when we imagine things that exist but are not perceived; while time is what we conjure up when we imagine such things moving from one part of space to the next. From past to future space, from memory to conjecture, the very two stances that exclude space, either because they are no longer or because they are not yet in it. The contradiction of all this turns life into an unexplainable enigma. As Leibniz wrote to Clarke: 'Under the assumption that space be something in itself it is impossible to give the reason why God should have put the bodies at this particular place and not somewhere else.'

The now is the explanation – things befall because they are part of now; now lights them up, unites them like a lightning flash from the cloud of the future to the ground of the past. From time immemorial lightning has been the emblem of illumination; Eckhart explained why: when it strikes, all the leaves on the trees turn over to front it, men are twisted round to face it, to see nothing but it on the face of everything, to behold all things in its light.

The creation of the world takes place now as an eternal, instant destruction and recreation; it is not something that happened once upon a time, but is going on here and now all the time: the essence of life is displayed in metamorphosis. Lightning is a good simile because people and things struck by lightning undergo a strange change.

Prospect imposes cold, top-heavy duty – thou-shalts, hard struggles for what is willed, a heart of stone. Retrospect is even worse. The inheritance of the past is a hoard of stale longings, mad pride, ghostly revenges and guilty terrors.

The dismissal of the fretting, future- or past-oriented psyche is the condition for living in the present, as a sheer, glowing awareness. Nowness is metaphysical experience; both are ungraspable, undefinable: the present instant cannot be measured. Interest in the future persistence of one's self ceases when all this is realised; Emily Dickinson explained: 'Forever / is composed of Nows / 'Tis not a different Time / Except for Infiniteness and latitude of Home.'

In the Japanese variant of the Rip Van Winkle myth, the Sea-King's daughter takes her human husband, Urashima, to live with her in her realm, where time is suspended. She keeps his soul stopped up in a bottle. When one's soul is safely put away in a bottle, one experiences what Emily was writing about, and what Blake had explained:

> Every Time less than the pulsation of the artery
> Is equal in its period and value to Six Thousand Years
> For in this Period the Poet's Work is Done, and all the Great
> Events of Time start forth and are conceived in such a Period
> Within a Moment, a Pulsation of the Artery.

All methods of meditation seek to instil this idea of time, beyond the clashing doors of past and future. A table of oppositions is shown on pages 20-21. In scanning it up and down, letting the opposites merge, separate and merge again, fresh insights are acquired; new ways of escaping the twin-pincered bondage of time are discovered.

On the left-hand column runs the list of life-giving energies. They cannot be analytically described, but only intuited. On the column to the right are their opposites, the analysable, 'solid' realities, in which the shaping energies are spent and struck dumb. A switch from beta- to alpha-rays corresponds to a shift of emphasis from the right to the left-hand column – from past to future. The idea of time as flowing from the future to the past helps to transcend time. The concept is common among traditional societies. In certain African cultures the future is felt at one's back; the chest steers towards the past, towards the ancestors; the ribs encage the present.

In Quechua the future is what lies behind. Quechuas explain that remembering means seeing the past before one; the mind cannot see the future, so it must be behind one's back.

Even more than the idea of time flowing down from the future, the notion of time past and time future as symmetrical can be of use. One may consider oneself as their axis of symmetry, as the One that divides and unifies the two opposite series – numbers progressing to the infinite, and fractions diminishing to zero. Actually fractions are heading towards One, since Oneness comprises the negation of itself: zero is one minus one. Also, numbers are actually reaching towards Oneness, which contains them all, and is their virtual totality. The axis of symmetry is reality, poised between two self-reflecting, opposite and equivalent delusions:

FUTURE	PAST
Shiva the eternal dawn	Kalî the mighty devourer
Beginning forever	Remembrance and anticipation
(FINAL) CAUSE	EFFECT
Uncaused emergence	Verbalisation through oppositiveness
The heart	Mentation
POETRY	PROSE
TENDENCY TO THE LIMITLESS	THE LIMITING
$\to \infty$	$\to 0$

BEING AS SUCH	BEINGS
To be	All other, finite modes and times of 'to be', all other verbs
ESSENCES	THINGS
Shaping forms; imagining images	Shaped forms; imagined images
Rhythms, proportions	Matter
Archetypal dreams	Apparent realities
POTENTIALITY	ACTUALITY
SEMEN	WOMB
Purusha	Mâyâ, Prakṛti
MEANING	SYMBOL
THE WORLD IS IN ME	I AM IN THE WORLD
SPACELESS, TIMELESS AWARENESS	THE OBSERVER VERSUS THE OBSERVED
WEFT	WEB
UNIFICATION	MULTIPLICITY

The second pair of opposites in the list, cause and effect, may need some explanation, since they are based on an obsolete Scholastic teaching which attributes to creation a formal cause (that into which things are made, which is the universe); a material cause (what things are made of, in Vedânta *mâyâ*, the art of delusion); an efficient cause (that by which things are made: the Creator and his power or wisdom in the West, Shiva and Shakti in India, and, in general, the primordial dyad, opposition as such); and finally a final cause (that for which, in view of which, things were, are 'made', which can only be liberation, metaphysical experience, the return to unity). All the other causes are actually its effects, because liberation, the absolute now, answers and solves, annihilates all queries.

Metaphysical experience is prior to the physical experiences which it crowns, recapitulates, interrelates, explains, consumes and dissolves. It is therefore called a death-and-rebirth. It frees from all father, mother and sibling figures and finally from one's self. It releases both from one's personal dream-world and from the shared dreams of social life, from the hauntings of madness, and from the collective delusion of reality-oriented action, even from panic in the face of horror and death.

The here and now, however awful, liberates. Even the intolerable becomes an illumination when, in Emily Dickinson's words,

> 'Tis so appalling it exhilarates
> So over horror it half captivates.
> The soul stares after it
> Secure to know the worst leaves no dread more.
> Others can wrestle,
> Yours is done
> And so of Wo bleak dreaded, come
> and terror's free
> gay – ghastly Holiday.

6 The complex relationship and relatedness of madness and illumination

What is madness and what is sanity? Where lies the difference between delirium and truth, hallucination and reality?

What is a real thing to start with? 'Thing' in most Germanic languages means an assembly; hence: the matter under discussion, what is considered relevant by the political body. What is reality? The Latin *res* was simply an item of communal interest. Social opinion is a changeful chimera, swayed by madness no less than individual imaginations. There exist famous collective hallucinations and yet only what oversteps the common track (*lira*) is called a de*lir*ium.

Men love to be reassured and excited by the clash of opposites, madness and sanity, delirium and reality. Hear the arrogance in the voice that pronounces somebody, something 'mad'. And yet reality-bound sanity is a social figment; it will appear monstrously unreal as soon as it is thrown into a new perspective.

The 'reality-oriented' attitude (among its variants: 'responsible', 'adult' attitude) can be challenged at any moment – the cautious, inquiring manner of most academics and professionals, which sets the tone of the respectable press, would be the butt of derision in other quarters – especially in revolutionary chapters, the nuclei of future respectability. A regressive, uncritical receptiveness is the only paying attitude under dictatorships based on repetitive propaganda; schizoid mannerisms of speech denote the proper orientation in totalitarian societies and in avant-garde circles. In vast gatherings frantic posturings are encouraged and admired as much as an amused superciliousness is appreciated in exclusive society. Mongols, faithful to Genghis Khan's testament, will admit that a man's body be washed on only three occasions, birth, marriage and death; step out of their camp and cleanliness becomes a near synonym of sanity, filth a symptom of derangement.

'Scientific' is so reassuring, and at the turn of the century it was the thing for a scientific-minded person to clip hysterical girls' clitorises and to shower everybody with radium.

Anybody not dulled by habit would feel about average social sanity the way Hopi boys at the turn of the century felt when subjected to modern schooling; one emerged to tell the story: 'I could name the States in the Union with their capitals, repeat the names of all the books in the Bible, quote a hundred verses of scripture, sing more than two dozen Christian hymns and patriotic songs, shout football yells, swing my partners in square dances . . . and tell dirty stories by the hour.' Don Talayesva in *Sun Chief* gives this neat, blood-curdling summary of what social sanity was, and, with inessential omissions and adjuncts, still is.

Idiocy, imbecility, paranoia, schizophrenia – they seem deadly ultimates in most places, but nobody dares apply them to their most obvious illustrations in a modern art gallery. Flippant smirks from all around would there throw off his balance the most ardent believer in sanity.

One's angle of vision should be rapidly and constantly shifted to different times and spaces, till the mind ceases to react automatically to the emotional charge of words denoting insanity and shame. To be pelted with insults at meetings was the first exercise in political adulthood for a Roman politician. To be despised as insane was a proof of devotion among certain Byzantine ascetics.

Even mere physical health is not an ultimate. Health to an American Plains Indian meant that he slept naked in the snow under the cold stars and during the day marched with the sun, for weeks and weeks on end, taking in his stride the slippery plain of ice and the rugged stony climb in turn, living off a handful of pemmican and clear water, disdaining to notice wounds that might set others raving. It is our social conventions that exclude from normality the habit of getting into different states of being, such as those into which boys and men in Bali can switch themselves so as to cease feeling pain when krisses penetrate their muscles; boys and men in parts of southern India normally fire-walk at the feast of Subrahmanya.

Christians stopped taking their doctrine seriously at an early date, otherwise they should stand by the taxing list of accomplishments incumbent on a normal believer, which the Master imparted on approaching the eleven to offer his last, summarising pronouncement. For a few lustrums at least people must have lived up to it: 'And these signs shall follow them that believe: in my name shall they cast out devils, they shall speak with new tongues; they shall take up serpents; and if they drink any deadly thing, it shall not hurt them; they shall lay hands on the sick, and they shall recover.'

All our assumptions waver when we dare to look systematically into the possibilities of a body attuned to intense feelings and expectations. Dare we commune with the mystic? To him ills are blessings, words whispered by God out of love, to be greeted with joy. Even non-dual Vedânta can make of pain the gateway to bliss. The case of Jadabharata is akin to the feats of early Christian martyrs. He became so distant from his body that he took whatever food was offered, sweetly bore offences and injuries, obeyed anybody's behest; like a leaf in the wind he let himself be drawn to the altar of Kalî to be sacrificed to her (of course she smote the sacrificers in time).

So the opposition of health and illness cannot hold good. Metaphysics provides us with the only true criteria, but they discourage contrastive thinking; in fact they stress blendings. Metaphysics would suggest that physical health be defined as the state of the body that allows the psyche to open up to the sheer awareness of being – and sanity as the condition of a psyche that ultimately tends to become sheer awareness. The distinction is neat, but by the terms of the definition even signs of death can be healthy, if they occasion enlightenment. Metaphysical experience transcends opposites and whoever pursues it will place health and morbidity in a metaphysical perspective, adopting or rejecting either – or rather, the conditions that go under their name – according to expediency, in view of the goal. Jung stressed that Buddhists favour hallucinations and make elaborate works of art of them, with the aim of breaking the crust of aimless social sanity. Even dissociation and schizophrenia proper, he noted, are used in meditation.

Fables preserve the tradition of insanity and downright folly as the best road to the highest form of sanity; for example, in the cycle of the unpromising hero, and in that of the worst possible choice (of a casket or of a horse). Percival is a mad youth, and only such innocence as his can save the kingdom from spiritual drought.

Visions of helpers and demons, of otherwordly domains, can be metaphysically valuable, because they release from the limitations of the actual. There is no reason therefore to remain stuck in the crude opposition of the imaginary and the real. Iranian metaphysicians found a neat philosophical formula to explain how things stood at this point of attainment: their 'imaginal level' is a reality with its own peculiar laws, having nothing to do with the arbitrary productions of fancy.

The metaphysical point of view imposes what on a lower level might seem very much like cynicism. The afterlife, reincarnation, legions of invisibles, cosmogonies – are all true, in the original sense of Old English treow, trustworthy, if they help to reach metaphysical experience. For Vedânta everything apart from metaphysical experience is a delusion, so it matters little which kind of delusion be used. Shaky creatures need crutches to approach the sacred well.

Some need a code of laws, others a revered class of persons to look up to; like tiresome children they want to know who and what is good or bad in the first place. Others need to brood on scenes of a collapsing world, like schizophrenics in their final stages, so why deny them nice prophecies about imminent catastrophes and millennia? Others manage to shake the problem of 'unmerited' suffering from their minds only by construing a system of give and take through several lives.

From a metaphysical perspective, most mental ailments are only a sign that the sufferer has ventured to raise, without knowing exactly what he is doing, metaphysical questions. The right guidance was lacking. Mental illness is the shadow cast by the idea of illumination. The insane one had the pluck to knock at the door leading to the higher levels of being, at least in his dreams, and now he pays for his daring. The unworldliness of metaphysical experience can seem terrifying, and the unfortunate, the aborted sage is granted only the preliminary purgation.

A healing process is a realisation of all this. It interprets symptoms as similes. The archetype of healing is shamanic initiation, in which sufferings are the prelude to elevation and revelation. Once the meaning of obsessions and compulsions is unveiled, the illness becomes a sequence of signifiers deprived of their significance, which fall apart. The moment this happens there is a cleavage, and in the intermission illumination, a sight of the fountainhead of significance, is granted.

Madness always implies a reckless but truthful connection with metaphysical experience; it obliges the patient and his keepers to face urges that ordinary callousness hides and dulls. So everything touching on the ultimate is usually avoided. Supreme questions are in bad taste. It is dangerous to see through the common, adaptable run of life; non-dual truth, from the point of view of duality, is sheer chaos. When a chink in the wall discloses what lies beyond, at once some ideology or delirium must be rushed in to close the gap. But a moment of revelation, a brief view through the cleft *has* been granted. The sick person does not escape his prison fate, but in the shift, from the cell of apathy to that of delirium, through a slit, he *does* make lightning contact with metaphysical truth. The paranoiac who suddenly intuits his iron system, the schizoid who for the first time lets himself flop into stupor, may feel the sort of revelation that Dostoevsky says he was granted during an epileptic fit.

If later the illness is overcome, it shall again be thanks to truth; the moment the paranoic order is shattered, or the dull mist of schizophrenia lifts, once again metaphysical truth flashes, once more the patient catches a glimpse of the source of all changes: the unwobbling pivot of peace *and* subversive source of disorder, oneness.

Mental diseases are attempts to fathom the deepest truth. Schizophrenia with its apathy overreacts to the question of how open one should be to outer suggestions. Paranoia envisages a circular explanation of the world. Deliriums are defences against the hidden chaos of ordinary reality. Sensing a kind of foreignness about one's inner processes or feeling one's thoughts hurtling through one's mind as though propelled by an alien force might all be insights into the exterior nature of mentation. What is wrong about the loss of the sense of the I in what used to be called amentia, apart from the accompanying distress? The bewilderment and estrangement of certain epileptoid conditions could be a fine metaphysical starter, and hysterical convulsive seizures, relaxing the body and making it impervious to pain, only lack a high motivation; many religious rituals induce them as a proof of a visitation from above. I asked a yoga master about the difference between the arousal of Kundalini and epileptic fits. The answer was: epileptic fits are bad Kundalinis. Schizophrenia discloses the most profound metaphysical truths, such as the fact that it is Unity that imparts unity even to the most trivial units of existence; that things do not exist in themselves, prior to an unconscious assumption of Unity. In the absence of metaphysical experience, this truth is unbearable, and the patient who is confronted with the experience of it, and discovers that there is no face in front of him, but only an eye, an ear, a wisp of hair, a pore, falls into stupor or becomes terrified. Those details appear gigantic, overwhelming. The reason is that they are billows from the ocean of bliss. The patient is like the child who takes the fierceness of mating for the fury of murder.

From a metaphysical point of view nothing is pathological. Not in the trivial sense that everything has a good side to it or that ultimate evil does not exist, but because duality is inherently false. There are mental derangements which no one could justify while remaining mentally alive, such as popular entertainments in industrial nations, and their high-flown counterpart, the avant-garde; and yet even in these a non-dual way of thought might read the lesson of Oneness.

The psyche of a people willingly immersed in the atmosphere of modern popular entertainment is that of children terrified by mother or father or sibling figures who follow no meaningful pattern and therefore tend to dilate into nightmares; to block the frightening development of gods into gorgons, the child becomes wilfully stunted, cuts even inwardly a low figure, pretends to be predictable. Idiotic entertainment helps in this kind of psychological trick. At its root is the need for quiet and loving modes of existence, which has been hopelessly thwarted.

In its terminal phase the avant-garde developed meaningless strings of words, faltering dialogues wading through mental haze. Something of the sort was also being tried out in hospital wards. The best approach with psychotic children proved to be a sign-language and a confused, confusing game of words seeking for a vague, tremulous significance, with meaning kept at a minimum, in an endeavour to encourage the child's tentative, dazed attempts at symbolisation. One ends up with Marianne Moore's verses in mind:

> Reading it, however, with a perfect contempt for it, one discovers in
> It, after all, a place for the genuine.

The psyche, a slippery reptile, will sneak out of the most elaborate traps. A generation brow-beaten into degradation, drugged, drawn into satanism around 1968, wriggled somehow out of it all and emerged seeking for metaphysical experience – a generation of knightly questers.

The line between pathology and health, horror and bliss, agony and glee is vague; it defies all analysis, eludes all measuring rods. The idiot and the saint, the maniac and the man of knowledge and power are hard to tell apart. Into the outskirts of Oneness people in need of sharp distinctions, of identifying badges, had better not venture. Here there are no judges' seats for complacence and officiousness to occupy.

There was once upon a time a garden of bliss full of trees bearing fruits of all kinds. Of one of the trees the fruits were forbidden. It was the tree-of-the-knowledge-of-good-and-evil, the opposite of the tree-of-identification-with-life, of ecstasy. Eating of the first tree, man became crafty like the gods, the forces of restriction and coercion (the Elohim), because he learned through the knowledge of good and evil to play one against the other, merge one with the other, extract one from the other; he opened his eyes, and became attached to things. But he paid for the power by becoming ashamed of his nakedness, of his simplicity, and the oneness of everything embarrassed him.

Who can stand being deprived of the power to coerce being, to mete out punishments and prizes, to fix tags on things?

Fancy wallows in court-room scenes, but for the mean pleasure of jurisdiction one pays by becoming awkward in bliss.

Yet in the garden of everyone's heart the need for Oneness, for bliss, is implanted.

Many bend under the strain; the pull of unity and the contrary drag of multiplicity are too much to bear.

What is it that harasses disturbed minds?

As always in criminal matters, the least suspect is the guilty. The diseased psyche is unsettled precisely by the idea of perfect health and bliss. Perfection perfected, Oneness is the torture of imperfection. The psyche that preconsciously knows all about perfection is upset at its failures to stand up to the standard. An inkling of what stands above upsets balances established at a lower level. To blot out the knowledge of bliss, perceptiveness itself is blunted. All that departs from Unity is a testimonial to Unity.

This also holds good with society at large.

There is no separation between individuals and societies; man is inwardly divided into many persons, and societies are somehow units.

From a metaphysical angle deliriums and ideologies, creeds of all sorts, are indistinguishable, save that the former happen to lack political power, fail to possess a sufficient number of minds; given a chance, there is nothing that cannot become the staple of social order, and probably nothing exists that has not been granted public honours somewhere at some time in history. Everything that is revered will one day seem something to be wiped out of the world for dear life. History delights in alternating between extremes. This is why it is worthwhile studying: it can free from the clutches of the historical.

Any set of ravings might become a social tenet. When this happens sooner or later the patient sages, who on the sly cultivate metaphysical truths, get busy adapting the dominant rigmarole, rearranging, reinterpreting it by dint of symbolism and casuistry, till it is woven into a veil of allegory and thrown over metaphysical truth. The way to weave the veil is to use the various parts of the delirium as reminders of metaphysical ideas; the funniest story of a mountebank visited by angels or of a bull butchered by the sun's child may serve as a memorial to the sacrifice of Oneness in multiplicity, and even a system of general mnemonics covering the whole universe of possible ideas can be developed out of it. The story remains a delirium to anybody not silly enough to share it and feel moved by it, or not wise enough to take for good its forced connection with the supreme experience of oneness. So ravings and posturings, once turned into allegory, may shock into timelessness.

7 Unity

The idea of unity, and the unifying, metaphysical experience it implies, are the premise of all order and meaning. First of all in the realm of numbers: apart from the many possible definitions, the idea of number is reached through the very same process of abstraction that leads to metaphysical experience, by stripping being of all its qualities, both essential and incidental. Numbered objects are stripped, in the numbering, of all their characters. Numbers are extensions or parts of Oneness. From One two series develop, the first tending to endlessness, the other to zero. The two opposite sequences are symmetrical manifestations or modifications of Unity – which potentially comprises both of them and is therefore infinite. It also comprises the idea of balance, since it contains all possible numbers. It implies the idea of equality and immutability, being equal to itself ($1 = 1$) and being also the standard of reference (1).

I was once told by an African Sufi the story of the jokes of One: 'If you pay homage to Him, repeating His name, He shows you His power and adds up. If you try to divide, penetrate and analyse Him, He remains impervious. If you try to multiply Him, He rejects all multiplicity and shows his unchangefulness. If you deny Him and try to subtract from Him, He plays a trick on you. He pretends to disappear, but you discover that He is all round you, encircling you; $1 - 1 = 0$.'

One is generative since it manifests-creates the series of numbers tending to the endless; and it is destructive, since it manifests-creates the decreasing, fractional quantities tending to zero. It comprises therefore all opposites and also their solution: itself. Since one is the triad (a) of itself, (b) of its specular image or symmetry aspect, and (c) of itself as the measure or criterion or axis of symmetry of (a) and (b), *oneness* corresponds to the triad of knower, known and knowing.

In one there is a three and the three is a return to one, but, since it does not exist in itself and by itself, it is a new one, a four. All successive numbers are successive leaps back to oneness. Metaphysical experience – which is the experience of Unity – comprises all numberable experiences, as light includes all the colours of the rainbow.

Numbers are beyond space and time. Order in space depends on a spaceless unit in space, somehow in space but not of space: the idea of the unextended point. Order in time depends on a timeless unit in time, somehow in time but not of time: the idea of the indivisible, immeasurable instant.

The point cannot be quantified, and is therefore Unity in space, containing all possible extensions. By extending itself it forms a line, straight or curved, and hence creates surfaces, dimensions.

The Unity of time lies in the split second, the caesura between two minimal ticks, the indivisible instant; diving into it, timelessness is reached. When one succeeds in wedging oneself into the interval between the instant jabs of pain, one ceases to feel it. Its continuance is unbearable, because one is chained to time. The wounded feel the injury and collapse only when they start to connect. In deep meditation the same suspension of continuity as experienced with drugs is achieved. Disconnected instants do not produce suffering, because they are each of them a unit and Unity cannot be unbalanced, racked, pained. Pain is precisely the linkage of each painful instant mirrored in the antecedent one; their specularity causes the expectation of a subsequent mirroring. The frightening perspectives of symmetry they cast on the future, the reduplications of each needle-unit of pain cause the suffering, which repeats the primordial symmetrical division *and* extension, the first sacrifice of unity – the pang of Creation.

With each stab isolated, their connection cut, the chain of pains snaps and each unit is unity: being, knowledge and bliss in one.

In space and time there is nothing that is not subject to change, to movement. The agent of movement is force – a measurable impulse which is Unity in action, the same Unity which as a one generated the measuring numbers; as a spaceless point generated the lines and surfaces of space; as a timeless instant generated the process of time; and which, once more as a number, as a unit, measures the ratio of space and time as speed.

The force of affinity – of love – is manifested unity returning back to itself as unmanifested. The force of affinity causes the cohesion of all bodies, both subtle and gross, psychic and physical. They are all manifestations of static unity in active unity – of unity in diversity. The force or unit of subtle, psychic reality is the ontological monad, or selfhood, which contains its own total possible development or destiny, and apprehends reality incidentally from the senses, but essentially from the source of reality: Oneness.

The monad coincides with the archetypes of all healing, the perfect, universal or cosmic man. On the subtle, imaginative and emotional level of reality, the cosmic monad is the equivalent of the point in geometry, of the instant in chronology, of force in the physics of gross bodies, of oneness in mathematics.

Metaphysical experience is the full realisation of static unity. It therefore offers the first premise or basic axiom of arithmetics, geometry, chronology and physics. It supplies the general idea of the specific indivisible units of which these systems consist, an idea that can be realised only in *asamprajñasamâdhi*, as an intellectual intuition. To those who choose to ignore this possibility, oneness, points, instants, forces, monads are but figments and paradoxes. On the contrary, indivisible, static unity is the reality of realities, which can be apprehended only with the utmost intellectual intensity – in *asamprajñasamâdhi*. Zeno symbolised the progressive degrees of intellectual tension as an open hand: sensation, fingers bent; critical assent, a clenched fist; understanding, a fist held by the other fist: true knowledge, in which the knower and the known merge with the intensity and compactness of a sharp, cleaving flame.

Unity as a word should be the most comprehensive word, the omnicomprehensive word, *the* Word.

Applied to the beginning of the Gospel of John, this identification makes metaphysical sense of the prologue. Replace word or *logos* with Oneness and the text opens up.

In language metaphysical experience can be identified with the seminal element, the verb, in respect to which adjectives are present or past particles, nouns are substantivated adjectives, and minor modifiers are chopped-up nouns. Of all verbs, only one can denote static unity, the one that is not of motion but of station: to be. 'Be' in itself and by itself in the infinitive tense denotes timelessness: the One. To be on the one hand contains, on the other negates whatever was, is, shall or might be.

As the copulation of past and present which is timelessness is symbolised in the vegetable and animal world by seeds, which contain both past and future, in language it is betokened by the copula of subject and predicate – the verb 'be'.

No word can speak the truth, but can only signify clusters of forms, images, dreams, with the one exception of 'be'. In their copula subject and object transcend their opposition and clash.

To convey metaphysical experience in words, one may starch and stiffen up the word 'be', meditate on it, till it becomes oneself.

Languages that omit the verb be stress its presence all the more: they resemble megalithic masonry, that placed the well-fitted stones one upon the other, each one pressing against the next, needing no mortar to hold them together. The tacit link of subject and predicate is even better than the actual verb 'be' as a symbol of the lightning flash that locks and illuminates the two poles of an action, creating a phrase. Words are shrunken phrases, compressed riddles. The Word then is 'Be'. All words imply that they *be*, as all realities imply metaphysical experience.

What is true of the language of words, holds good with all idioms – music, dance, gestures, sculpture, painting.

In music the copula is silence, in dance immobility, in sculpture and painting empty space. In the special case of icons it is the gold-leaf background.

Apart from offering in 'be' the symbol of Oneness, languages are nothing but textures of metaphors, of conveyances. In Greek *metaphora* is 'means of transportation'. Metaphors carry us away from immediate reality and no appeal to the metaphor of grit or groundrock can re-cross the gap. Belief in the existence of privileged, ultimate, factual, non-digressing, non-metaphorical metaphors is a childish conjuration.

Schizophrenic regression pretends that some words denote objects and not classes. A gritty rock-bottom 'basic reality' does exist, but it is not a special code, a magic string of words; it is the merger of knower and known, and the various languages are games of delusion staged to cover up its silence. The less we take them seriously, the less we identify with them, with their pretence of coinciding with reality, the truer we are. We shall also be more apt at translating codes if we privilege none. If there is a suggestion arising from metaphysical experience, it is playfulness, the dalliance of the Godly Youth. Descriptions of reality are the toys of the all-wise child Dionysus. It is in a Dionysian linguistic intoxication that truth is best approached.

Synonyms and similes of expansion and greatness are then poured forth, a spiralling rhythm urges on the flow of metaphorical inventiveness until words are propelled by an unknown, transcendent force, and metaphors pile up, more and more far-fetched, the idiom becoming richer and richer, the intoxication mounting, and the distance between 'the sparkle of words' and individual reality narrowing in a spiral.

Shamans command a vocabulary far more extensive than the ordinary; they are drugged with similes. In dealing with the intermediary world, only poetry will prevent symbols from turning into signs, nudges into definitions, living life into lived life. Rhythmic, gushing metaphorical creations, overspilling similitudes, should in the end break the habit either of turning to three-dimensional solids for precision, certitude and truth or of seeking for certainty in one's own person, in the limits of individual life. Wordsworth explained:

> Our destiny, our being's heart and home
> Is with infinitude, and only there.

Only apart from one's shape and name one can reach truth. I

remember a man intellectually honest; he snapped at his lover when she dared call him by his name.

What makes us real is our need to be a monad, which is impossible insofar as we coincide with our personal equation: our name and shape. Shakespeare explained this in *Richard II* (V. v. 38):

> But whate'er I be,
> Nor I nor any man that but man is,
> With nothing shall be please'd till he be eas'd
> With being nothing.

Absolute individuality and absolute universality coincide in the monad of metaphysical experience; this cannot be 'touched' by *sober* words. Words as such are signifiers that cannot signify significance itself, what lies before, above and beneath the opposition of a signifier and a thing signified, of likeness and difference. Oneness, as absolute universality and absolute individuality, is both cosmic and non-dividual. It is the absolute here and now.

At the peak of metaphysical experience, of utter silence and unity, the meaning of all things is revealed, in the sense that, once reached, the need and quest for factual reality is seen through and ceases. It is on this level that the principles or axioms of every form of knowledge are intuited, not constructed; not deliberately posited, but experienced: the point, the monad, force, the eternal instant, absolute infinity.

All that is not at this level is unreal, not reality-giving, according to Vedânta; it possesses being like the snake for which one has mistaken a rope – only by virtue of the rope and only so long as it is not discriminated from the rope. If we prefer Leibniz to Shankara we may say that bodies, things extending in space, are not substances but appearances, because only a principle of unity, a shaping form, a point of view on the universe will lend a semblance of substance to their unsubstantial multiplicity, 'as with rainbows and mock suns'.

This is best conveyed by analogy. Ibn 'Arabî tells the story of how King Solomon suggested unsubstantiality to the Queen of Sheba: by showing her into a room with a crystal pavement. She took it for water and lifted her skirt so as not to wet it. When she saw that there was no water, she suddenly understood that all reality is a game of likeness and difference and that the world is annihilated and recreated at every tick of the clock.

It sometimes happens that the truth slips into one's mind when one sees oneself unexpectedly full-size in a mirror. The instant one meets oneself as a stranger the revelation is granted. It sometimes happens to people who, on the eighth or ninth day of typhus, think they see their own body lying at their side.

Borges insists on the experience of the mirror in a poem about

> . . . the impenetrable crystal
> where an impossible space of reflections
> ends and starts, uninhabitable.

He explained in an interview that in boyhood he one day panicked at his own image in the looking-glass, fearing it might move on its own, against his will. In such cases one *sees* the absurdity of man's prime error, identifying with his body, and soul.

Illumination beyond madness and sanity leads to what Guru Narayana, the Kerala Vedantic master, described in a poem:

> *You* are the Absolute, you are not your senses, not your thoughts,
> Not your intelligence, not your consciousness, not your body,
> Life itself and you yourself, you are both unreal.
>
> . . .
>
> The manifest world is nothing apart from you,
> It is your self that glitters like a mirage all around you.
>
> . . .
>
> What emanated nature, what pervades and compacts it,
> The enjoyer of its variety, and the I of deep unconscious sleep,
> The self-existent, constant bliss,
> Perfection perfected – all this, listen! you *are*.

This is *total* paranoia, *absolute* schizophrenia, *complete* intoxication, the tuning-fork of sanity: unity.

II *Archetypes*

8 Numbers as archetypes

Metaphysical experience realises infinite oneness. Oneness reflects, mirrors itself, and by so coming back to itself avers its oneness as a new One, which is two, and so on, progressively becoming all further numbers. Each number is a return to oneness: being a unit, it is a homecoming of One. It would not exist if it were not a manifestation, a type of oneness. In the production of numbers as with the lever, elevations are due to downward pressures. This backward-running, crab-like genesis of numbers haunted Emily Dickinson; she felt that it concealed a lesson in the essence of life, the great ancient lesson: that true totality or infinity is Oneness undivided, unmultiplied, and that all twoness or multiplicity is delusion and falsity. In moments of ultimate finality we are alone: all One. Within One everything is every other thing, symmetry is absolute, consciousness as binary, contrastive logic disappears. On One consciousness may only border, as a marginal consciousness on the point of melting into the unconscious. In the *Mahâbhârata* (XII) the paradox comes often to the fore: in *samâdhi*, one hears not, smells not, tastes not, sees not, perceives no touch, one's mind forms no resolve, desires nothing – one is like a stick, a stump, a stone, a flame in a windless place. No consciousness is left, in the sense that no duality subsists. One passage says that 'unity results only when one is not conscious *with* consciousness'. There exists an awareness paradoxically without consciousness, in the characterless, non-dual unity as 'seen by the *substance* of consciousness, by the *light* of the mind', as though by the remembrance of unification in the unity of Oneness. One is literally *absorbing*. Emily dared express the experience of it:

One and One – are One.
Two – be finished using.
Well enough for schools
But for minor choosing –
Life – just – or Death
Or the Everlasting.
More – would be too vast
For the Soul's comprising.

(Incidentally, the detail will add depth to the poem: in the first version, instead of 'minor' she wrote 'inner', and instead of 'more', 'two'.)

Among numbers some are more One-like, more life-or-death- or everlastingness-like, Emily would say, than others; and they have the property of unifying, ordering the other numbers into sets, which make it possible to calculate and assort vast amounts of them. One-like numbers are the units of measure, the archetypes. Ten, the archetype of decimalisation, is the most known, and, among Pythagoreans, revered.

In One all numbers, infinite new ones, are potentially comprised. In an archetypal number such as ten not all numbers, but an infinity of tens are latent. Between oneness – absolute infinity – and finite numbers, the relative infinities or archetypes mediate.

In geometry, angles, being relative infinities of space, mediate between the point, in which all of space is latent, and finite geometrical figures. Monads, which are a qualified infinity of time, the time of a person in its uniqueness, mediate between the instant, in which all time is latent, and finite chunks of history, periods of time.

Fields of energy, which structure a relative infinity of movements, mediate between force, which contains the infinite potential movements, and particular movements defined by a given speed and vector.

In languages modifiers, which establish modes, time, and case, mediate between the infinitive of being – 'to be' – and single words.

The primal, creative notion or emanation of Oneness is a self-mirroring, which is both an intellectual reflection and a purposive action. It is the primal force and the original identity since it is identity-giving. All movements derive from the impulsion of the primal force, all thoughts are reflections of the original act of self-reflection. The usual definition of a person is: a synthesis of intellect and will, of reflection and action. So it seems correct to call the first motion of Oneness the Knower – to consider it a person. Self-knowledge on the part of Oneness means that Oneness divides into Oneness as the Known and Oneness as the Knower. The Known is all, infinite being. The Knower is all knowledge and can therefore be styled 'Cosmic Intellect' or 'Active Intellect' or 'the Word'. The Known and the Knower involve a homecoming of both to unity as such: the Known and the Knower unite in the knowing. The homecoming to unity answers the definition of bliss. Vedânta speaks of the primal triad of being, knowledge and bliss.

These archaic thoughts may seem funny, but only by accepting them does one gain a metaphysical standing above the round of days. A sage remarked that nobody knows God – the Absolute – any more since nobody will stoop low enough. Low enough to detect the distinction between the primary motion of Oneness, which creates the first triad, and the next move, which is latent in the first, whereby oneness, coming back to itself, revolving spirally on itself, forms a new One. This new One is a relative oneness, since it subsists only by virtue of its relation to the triad; and is also a second One: two. One should stoop low enough to see the prime symbol of this metaphysical truth in the primal unity of mother and child, with the bond of air, breath-spirit and/or the nipple to make a triad, which will develop in the second oneness, the child, who first realises (the loss of) the nursing couple and next notices itself as a second One.

The Knower is originally the realisation of symmetry in oneness; next He becomes a two and more, multiplying-dividing both Himself into Knowers and the Known into things, descending to computations of numbers, measurements of forms, reckonings of time, calculations of velocities and vectors. Originally the Knower is all-knowing. We can try to realise this premise, if not by identifying with it, then by considering approximations to it, such as the illuminations of prophets or of poets like Valmiki, who grasped the whole of the Ramâyâna in a flash. Or we may realise it by returning to the prime symbol of the child who knows all that need be known, being one with the mother.

The Knower, in his scattering of himself into multiplicity, multiplies the Known whose reflections He is. He is apparently split into myriad reflections of Himself, which illuminate and tip off the workings of brains, of human machines. The presence, the ray, the force of the Knower is manifested, betrayed in infinite bodies. Relay and betray come from the same Latin root; *trad*ition and be*tray*al are inseparable twins. Sheer, faultless thought, the precise measurement, is the Knower made manifest, relayed: his Word. The human being plays host to Him, but beyond this it should not venture. All it can do on its own is make blunders, betray.

The descent into multiplicity is possible only through mediators standing between the Knower and the multitude of numbers-numbering-numbered-things, since only through the mediation of relative infinities – archetypes, units of measure – can the absolute condescend to the finite. They are the preconditions of all numeration and limitation, and cannot therefore be found by means of calculation or accord to rigid definitions. Being specifiers they cannot be specified. The intuition of archetypes mirrors metaphysical experience and thereby coincides with it, but insofar as the intuition of the archetypes is not the experience mirrored, but the act of mirroring, it is distinct, separate and fragmented, unmetaphysical. Standard numbers – archetypes – mirror numbers because they unify sets of ordinary numbers; but whereas one multiplied by one makes one – because one does not contain multiplicity – units of measure are subject to multiplication, because they contain multiplicity, ambiguity, relativity.

A number becomes a standard or archetype by symbolising, standing for unity; but the reason why this holds good is not logically cogent and analysable, since cogency resulting from analysis is a type of computation effected by the use of a standard or archetype. The only type of 'reason' that can be given for adopting an archetype – a reason-giver – is a feeling of analogical fitness akin to taste, sympathy, discretion.

Going back once more to the seed-plot of symbols, which is the primal stage of a child's growth, the archetypes come into play as soon as the mother communicates to the child the right measure of absorption, circulation and expulsion – the old triad of being, knowing and bliss back again. The mother passes on the archetypes especially in those moments in which the prior unity of mother and child as nursing couple is most warmly and closely evoked. Plato drew attention to the philosophical import of lullabies, and derived all healing procedures from them. One may add that they contain the whole range of the possible attitudes towards the archetypes in the form of distinct rhythms: the trend to multiplicity in the iambics ∪-, ∪-, which the mother uses to imitate the dispersal, the multiplicity, the torment of the child; she has thereby insinuated herself into its rhythmic web, after which she brings into play the archetype of the return to unity, slowing down, softening into trochees and dactyls - ∪, - ∪ ∪. The child's pulses, caught in the net of counter-imitation, follow the lead, and the mother can now bring into play a third stance: restful unification, slumber and ecstasy mirrored in stately, booming anapests ∪ ∪-, ∪ ∪-.

Like rhythm, numbers are also choice connoters of archetypes.

Calculations by pairs can mirror the symmetry aspect of Oneness, and therefore also the Knower, the Universal Intellect as the reflection, the Word, or the Mirror. Like all archetypes it is polar, both cohesive (all lines can be said to link their *two* extreme points) and disruptive (they can be said to separate them). Night is dark, but it lights up the language of the stars, which day blots out.

Bisecting and yoking, coupling, pairing, halving and doubling will not get one too far in calculations; but scores, the typical tally, can prove a valuable unit: fingers and toes together witness to it.

Threefold divisions are instructive because triads imply two extremes, with harmony and/or oddness, the trickster twilight, in between. All geometrical figures are multiple triangles, all colours are a mixture of the three primary ones, the character of a musical key is decided by its third note being major or minor. Man is three-ply, body, soul and spirit, and his disposition depends on his third part, the spirit, being uplifted or drawn down. For greater articulateness, triadists resort to ninefold divisions: Dante explains that Beatrice 'was a nine' – something to be hailed three times three

– a trinity squared. 'Nine' and 'new' stem from the same root. After nine months a new creature is born.

Multiplicity or materialisation begins only after Three, as an after-manifestation of Threesomeness. The Knower first reflects the Known as something new and next realises that the ensuing Knowing makes a total of Three-in-One, which is a new One, actually a four. The novelty of the fourth one consists in its being a manifestation of multiplicity as such. Beatrice was a new Three, not a four: she was *the* perpetual newness, not *a* circumscribed novelty; a direct embodiment of the Knower, not a multiple, delusive reality. Nine is the sum of any interval between two notes and of the interval resulting from their inversion – which though new and different remains unchanged, either consonant or dissonant, either major or minor. This purport of Nine – sameness in difference – can be heard when a musical interval is inverted to produce a second one; it can be seen in the most holy Hindu diagram, the *Shrî Yantra*, which is a series of concentric circles at whose centre nine triangles dynamically interpenetrate, five of them upward- and four downward-pointing, with an inversion both of number, from odd to even, and of direction. Their interplay draws the eye one-pointedly to the unchanging, unmarked, and all the more emphasised centre. Nine is the centring of the centre. The square that encloses the whole is fourfold, a Four. The rind around the ninefold core is a foursome. Nine, the Knower, ends in a four. Dynamic unity ends in stabilised, foursquare multiplicity. The Knower is quartered on the cross, appearing as the point that branches out in four perpendicular lines: the two diameters of the circle of manifestation. Four is the homecoming of One and at the same time Oddity itself, matter. There are three primary colours as such, but four pigments in the eye. Sets of fours square things with a sense of definiteness and repose, and sets of eights even more so – as can be seen in the octagonal bases of lingams, or in the lay-outs of baptisteries, and as can be heard in the all-important octave. When the ear hears the eighth note, it recalls the first one, and feels that they are identical and yet different. The eighth interval clinches the archetypal set of notes. Already the fourth interval, which is called subdominant, had charmed the ear, as though announcing the octave. The Egyptians felt that the octave was like the relation of spring to autumn, the squaring of accounts in the circle of the year.

In Japanese four is *Yo*, which also means 'the world'; eight is *Ya*, 'the house', which is a reflection of the cosmos.

Doubly eightfold was the liver, the reflection of the cosmos for the Etruscans. Also the Chinese felt that sixteen was the cosmic, four-square number. A pound is felt to be well squared in sixteen ounces.

Five marries divisible two and indivisible three, and like Oneness it cannot be divided; so it was the number of living nature. It recurs in the planetary rhythms of Venus-Morning-star. Since the fifth interval in music is the essence of harmony, the archetypal sense of the Egyptians felt it corresponded to the winter solstice in respect to springtime, when the five-petalled flowers bloom. A tune slides smoothly from one key to the next, if between the keys there is affinity, which means five intervals; all smooth handling, moulding and perceptive feel of objects is based on having them at one's five fingertips. In the eye the three primary colours are received by four pigments plus the black pupil. A double five is the totality of digits: nature's abacus. A double five is such a fountainhead of meanings that the decimal system is the archetype of archetypes, unity perfected: it is the sum of the first four numbers (1 + 2 + 3 + 4) and its half is the sum of the middle two (2 + 3).

In the Latin notation it forms the cross of St Andrew, the wheel, the hourglass. Two fives or hands or funnels or tents, joining, form a calix. Five points make a quincunx, the ideal form of plantations, the intersection of the zodiac and the ecliptic: X. The arabic notation 10 implies that two fives are unity perfected, revealing what precedes even unity: 0, mere possibility, the nothingness that unity-allness must comprise. Zero itself is the negation of number, 1 − 1. But when it is placed at the side of a number, 1 (1 − 1), and considered relative, it becomes a relative negation, negating the set of numbers to which that number belongs, hence affirming the following, successive set. 1 denotes absolute infinity, 0 absolute possibility; their junction is the manifestation of possibility, alias *the* relative infinity. 10 is *the* archetypal number, from tithes to decimations. In the 1 of 10 all the 9 manifestations are comprised, and they are shown to add up to 0. So 10 is the real, perfect

1, the full manifestation (1) of the unmanifest (0). In Vedic qualitative arithmetic as expounded by Bharati Krishna Târthaji, oneness, absolute and perfected as 10, becomes its own unmanifest, absolute Knower as 9 (3^2); then passes into possible manifestation as 8; manifests being as 7; reveals itself in oppositions, couplings, and beings as 6; is reflected in psychic matter, in images, as 5; becomes Air, the container of forms, as 4; turns into light and fire, the moulders of all forms, as 3; it dissolves all forms into water as 2; and finally appears as earth, the cohesive force 1; and thanks to the realisation of nothingness, 0, it becomes an archetype of totality, 10. From the apparent, earthly Oneness of concrete things, we proceed back through distillation, abstraction, and reach 2 (or $\frac{1}{2}$), the possibility of becoming anything, which is latent in everything, and which is symbolised by water; next comes 3 (or $\frac{1}{3}$), the passage from manifestation to the unmanifest, symbolised by fire. Next comes the unapproachable moulder of forms, the illuminator that turns everything into invisible air, which symbolises being itself by virtue of its all-pervasiveness: 4 (or $\frac{1}{4}$). We pass on to 5 (or $\frac{1}{5}$), imponderable reality, subtle being, the psyche or matrix of images; to 6 (or $\frac{1}{6}$), the primal duality or multiplicity, also symbolised by air; to 7 (or $\frac{1}{7}$), the manifestation of the unmanifest, symbolised by water, the solvent; to 8 (or $\frac{1}{8}$), the earth, bare possibility; to 9 (or $\frac{1}{9}$), the Knower of all things as units (1) returning to nothingness (0): as nothings (0) in respect to One (1), 10 (or $\frac{1}{10}$). 9 multiplied by any number gives a sum whose digits add up to 9. Divided by 1 the result is 9 forever recurring. In 9 reality is totally revealed.

All this implies that symbolically $1 = 9$, $8 = 2$, $2 = 8$, $7 = 3$, $6 = 4$, $5 = 5$. The point of reversal from gross to subtle being is the imagination, the psyche, which is the symbol of itself, being the symbol-maker. It is V – the neck of the hourglass X. Dividing 1 by 5 we obtain 0·2; 1 by 2 = 0·5.

With 5, which is the hand, the protector, the family, 6 can compete as an archetype, since it is the all-container, the Manifold as such. The four quarters of the horizon plus zenith and nadir make six, like the months from solstice to solstice. Six doubles into the number of the notes in the octave, of the chromatic scale, of the zodiac's round, wherefore one counts by dozens, and a foot is divided into twelve inches, and a shilling in twelve pennies. Gold is weighed by sets of twenty-four grains, which make a pennyweight, or by sets of twelve ounces, which make a troy pound. Multiply 6 by 10 and you can count the hours; by 60 and you count the days in the year, the degrees in the circle, the veins in the body, the seconds in the hour. Multiply the sides of a perfect triangle – $3 \times 4 \times 5$ – and 60 results. 60 was the Sumerian high God, to whom other gods-numbers were related as to Oneness.

Seven seems to serve as many archetypal turns – it is light born of fire, it is the limit of knowledge, of meaning, it is related to the measurer Moon, with the 28 lunar mansions corresponding to as many vertebrae in human bodies. It is indivisible, so in this respect too it recoils back to one; it is immobile and virginal because it generates nothing within the decade and is nothing's double, which makes it similar to zero, the ungenerated and ungenerating. It was fit as an archetype for the unidentical, primary notes; for the basic movements; for the seven stars round the lodestar and the seven openings of the heart; for minimal pregnancies; for illness up to the critical day; for intervals up to the first dissonance, as intolerable as the second; for planets up to the evil one; and a cycle ends at three score and ten, the number of a life's work concluded. In measuring the extent of memorisation, the limit of seven elements has been discovered to be the optimum.

Combining the numbers from 1 to 13 ($12 + 1$ or $10 + 3$ or $2^2 + 3^2$ which relates to $5 = 2 + 3$), all sorts of complexities unfold and the fundamental measures are found for all reality.

To think is to ponder, to weigh; to relate is to re-count; to judge is to gauge. One adds and subtracts, besides numbers, figures in space, periods in time, degrees in force, words in language, as Hobbes noted, since by adding names one affirms; by adding affirmations one syllogises and demonstrates, by subtracting implicit affirmations from conclusions the remaining are uncovered; by adding and subtracting laws and facts, right and wrong are disclosed: all thinking is reckoning. The swiftness of the operations conceals the calculations of instinct, of the sense of harmony and proportion in artists. Therefore every assessment is a calling down of archetypes, of units of measure that make the calculations possible and speedy: they are the trumps of the game, the scales of the music.

Archetypes are standards of measurement. Mental categories and basic emotional plexuses at the same time, they work on all levels. The grand truth that exalted Pythagoras was precisely the discovery of this relatedness of levels: a given harmony of sounds corresponds to a certain proportion in space, to a precise feeling in the heart. Plucking in a certain manner the cords of a lyre, one evokes a relationship of heights and lengths, a corresponding distribution of spaces; music is liquid architecture, sculpture or painting, as these are frozen music, and the soul testifies to the common structure of all.

Computations are possible by virtue of standard units, partitions of space are based on a basic proportion, evaluation of movements depends on rhythms, metrics, periodisations. Scales enable one to modulate music and grammatical modifiers to articulate thoughts, and finally timbres create the all-enfolding atmosphere, the flavour, the pervading essence, as George Eliot explained in *The Spanish Gipsy:*

> Speech is but broken light upon the depth
> Of the unspoken; even your loved words
> Float in the larger meaning of your voice
> As something dimmer.

Timbres, voices are in their turn archetypally divided and counted. Hindus distinguish the bosom-, tiger-, morning-voice; the throat-, goose-, midday-voice; the head-, peacock-, night-voice. Voices can also be fourfold or fivefold like the elements, or sevenfold like the planets, or zodiacally twelvefold.

Archetypes, which knit all levels together, answer to the range of inner promptings, which were called gods or angels and are now known either as psychic complexes or as supreme ideals, depending on whether at the moment they are on the make or clinging to power. The scenery of life is tinctured by them, it is interpenetrated and interpreted, scored or ignored, thrown into relief or flattened, according to the archetypes at play. Things depend on the tone that is set, and this depends on the units of measure that are adopted. That numerical archetypes trigger emotional plexuses is acknowledged in the *I Ching*, in games, especially cards, where they are the trumps, and in the superstitious reactions to 13 and 17, which have not yet been tucked under the carpet of consciousness. In Egypt there was a thirteen-month zodiac which took into account the precession of the equinoxes, hence the number 13 hints at sinister esoteric knowledge, at a standard of measure that puts everything into a different, unsettling perspective. In the Sleeping Beauty story of Little Briar Rose, the supernatural Women of Destiny are 13, but the King cannot invite them all because he has only 12 gold plates, so his newborn daughter pays for the slight. In the twelve-month year there are intercalary, interpolated, thirteenish days, when Saturn reverses all customs as Lord of Misrule. Besides, there is the critical, fishy, Pisces passage of Carnival, when the sun is old and has spent all of his twelve fecundating rays on the Moon. The legends vary. One set says that his son, Lucifer, takes his place and sacrifices himself for him, releasing the spring lightning, the thirteenth ray, that reawakens him or brings him back to life in Aries. But Lucifer is also Venus, or has a twin or is half man and half woman; Tommy and Dirty Bet represent the dual creature, Thirteen, the Sinister Saviour of the year.

Actually 13 is 12 + 1, the secret, the esotericism of 12. So the Tao-tê-Ching says, in Erkes's version:

> To step out into life means to enter death.
> The companions of life are thirteen
> The companions of death are thirteen
> Of deadly spots in the man striving for life there are also thirteen.

The addition of a one to scores, also totally changes the pitch of things – $12 + 1 \simeq 20 + 1$. Twenty-one is a multiplication of odds ($3 \times 7 = 21$). So paying in pounds or in guineas makes all the difference.

Musicians in refined civilisations, in Java or in Bali, pass the day adjusting the pitch; the evening concert will unfold in a natural unconcerned flow.

Iago snarls at Othello and Desdemona:

> O! you are well tun'd now,
> But I'll set down the pegs that make this music,
> As honest as I am.

Archaic supreme authority lay with the keeper of the calendar, the scale of festivals – the pegs on which all rituals hinged – from the tuning of the flutes to the evocations of the gods, to the ratios of exchange between types of money.

The fact that archetypes are fields of psychic energy and units of measure at the same time is certainly disconcerting, and he who can read one side of the coin is the kind of person who will refuse, will scarce be able to decipher the opposite one.

Every 25,920 years the sun changes sign in the zodiac, and 25,920 divided by the archmeasurer or Oneness of time, 60, yields 432. $60^3 = 216{,}000$ whose double is 432,000. Myths are spun round this number – 432 – all over the world, infusing it with the feeling and flavour of the relatively ultimate. 432 defines a cosmic era in India, connotes the Norse Valhalla at the end of the cycle, and Berosus gives the same figure for the extent of a Chaldean cycle; the lay-out of Angkor Wat testifies to the number, as *Hamlet's Mill* reveals. This does not mean that myths are mere accretions of numerical facts. They are the number's projection in the world of dreams, and man is rooted in dreams, so he truly understands the meaning of standard numbers only by determining their dream shadow, his corresponding secret inner stirrings.

A cubic clepsydra whose water eked out in twenty-four hours provided the standard measures in Babylon; its edges were the foot cube, its content was the standard volume, its weight the unit of weight.

Cybele was the Cube. She was the earthy Goddess of desire, the pitch of psychic intensity. And her 'sons' were metrical feet.

Quantities can thrill with their quality. This should not seem strange if we bear in mind the basic experiment of Pythagoras: when a chord is strung on a stick called *canon*, divided in 12 equal sections, the vibration of its whole length and of its half (of 12 and 6, 2/1) corresponds to the same note at the distance of an octave; the proportion of 12 and 8 yields the interval of five between the two notes. The pleasure that such intervals afford expresses numerical proportions. Numbers and emotions coincide.

9 The emotional perception of archetypes

What we actually perceive is ultimately decided on the archetypal, or what used to be called the divine level. Between now and the times in which the tuning of flutes and the carriage of participants in rituals were acknowledged to be the main affair of the State, the difference is not in the substance, but in the awareness. Matters archetypal are still supreme, but nowadays goals beyond the grasp of a generation have become too remote. Our minds can no longer seize the whole picture, nor follow the string of causes from the ordering units of the cosmos to the surrounding physical reality.

Physical reality is an assemblage of types, though one is deluded into believing that it is made of individual objects.

The Greek 'type' means mark, sign, imprint, image, form. Words denote types; to describe an individual, a concrete object, we arrange types in the unique required combination, as we calculate numerals until we obtain the exact serial number of an individual object, or as we combine types from the printer's set until they are arranged to form the needed word.

We are deluded into believing that 'concrete individual' is something beyond the combination of typical traits. But 'individual' means something indivisible, which is only true of metaphysical Oneness. True concreteness – in the sense of 'grown together' (*cum crescere*) into a unity, a monad – is not to be found in what words and types point at, but in the opposite direction, in what enables us to use and assemble meaningfully the finite words and types: in archetypes, that are relatively infinite, and that lead back to the primal source, *archê* itself, metaphysical experience. Only by transcending words, images, impressions, will-o'-the-wisps, does one touch truth: not by prizing the 'raw' impression above its 'baked' expression, but by realising that both are delusions and that truth lies in reaching the source of impressions and words – the archetype that gathers them into its mould. The archetype is the mover, it turns us towards the object and presents the object to us. If we reach towards the archetype that is the source of the appearance, the type of the object, and therefore its true meaning, we shall cease to seek for truth among appearances. We are not monads, except when we are beyond ourselves, immersed in metaphysical experience; usually we are an aggregate of fleeting impressions with the tag of a name attached. We do not see objects, but clusters of imprints. Impressions, imprints, are stamped with the seal of the ruling archetype of the moment, which gives the scene a relative unity.

We perceive what speaks, appeals to us. Either things signify or we do not notice them. Realities are metaphors, since everything conveys a meaning. This implies that everything depends on an archetype. Something utterly meaningless, not alerting an archetype, would not even be picked up by the senses.

The idea of human perception which should prevail, according to the experimenters Beer and Kugler, is that based on the behaviour of the *bacillum coli*, which, though devoid of memory, finds its way to its food in our bowels. It picks up the 'appeal' of food like an insect drawn into a cobweb. Its system of perception, like all others, including our own, but more obviously so, feels the invariance of structures, the information that remains unchanged over variations in time and space. The invariances in the flux are picked up, particularly those that affect the psyche, and evoke a response on the archetypal, dream-world level.

Facts shadow forth dreams. Happenings in the world of visible bodies are reflections of events on the archetypal level. What about wounds and beatings? They seem solemn enough reminders of the importance of tangible facts. But who would inflict them if it were not to psychically dispossess, or exorcise the victim? It is because of the meaning that is lent to wounds that one inflicts them. The vanquished kiss the hands of the victor because of a subtle compulsion, not only out of cowardice. To them victory 'is' a 'favour of the gods' – not only a brutal fact.

There is no such thing as an event in itself; death itself can 'be' a passage to real life and an occasion for rejoicing, or a crude, irredeemable, despairing destruction; pain can 'be' an eagerly coveted badge of honour, or a spicing for lust, or a means of transcending fear and worldliness, or else just distressing waste and horror. It all depends on the dreams into which death or pain are fitted, on the meaning that is projected on them, animalised in them. Appeals to gritty reality or to a foolproof standard of sanity are hollow exorcisms of the overruling power of the archetypes. Ideas of reality and standards of sanity are dreams.

All we can do, when dreams collide, is try and translate one into the other, knowing that there is no code of codes above them.

Truth lies not in the object, whose essence is perceivability, nor in our consciousness of it, in the fact that we are awake rather than dreaming. When one seeks truth in apparent objects or in the waking apprehension of appearances, one is rebutted.

To some this is strangely irritating. They invoke the inescapable evidence of 'this table and chair'; they even kick, like Doctor Johnson in refutation of Bishop Berkeley's evidence. Hypnotisers often come across such patients, who flaunt their belief in sound facts, and insist on taking 'this table and chair' for undeniable ultimates. Milton Erickson recommended that one concernedly listen to them, and then lead them on and on, insisting on scrutinising the objects they point to, making them expand on the patent absurdity of denying such undeniables, interrupting them now and then to protest that one wants to understand them better and better, inviting them to digress about the more or less tense bodily attitude that goes with the proper, level-headed acceptance of reality. Once the dependence on the hypnotiser's questioning is established the apostolic realist will easily drift into hypnotic sleep, during which 'this table and chair' can be turned into anything. The archetypal builders of 'reality' Blake called Ulro and Los:

> As to the false appearance which appears to the reasoner
> As of a Globe rolling thro' Voidness, it is a delusion of Ulro.
> The Microscope knows not of this nor the Telescope: they alter
> The ratio of the Spectator's Organs, but leave objects
> untouch'd.
> For every space larger that a red Globule of Man's blood
> Is visionary, and is created by the hammer of Los
> And every Space Smaller than a Globule of Man's blood opens
> Into Eternity of which this vegetable Earth is but a shadow,
> The red Globule is the unwearied Sun by Los created
> To measure Time and Space to mortal Men every morning.

Whatever challenges our senses with a claim to truth, meditation will strip to its inescapable delusiveness. Meditation on reality necessarily comes up against a curved wall; one is compelled to retrace the origin of the perceived and the perceiver in an archetype and this leads back to metaphysical experience. Only by inverting our thrust, by revoking our faith in the 'painted veil', can we approach truth, through the gateway of archetypal experience, turning away from appearances to apparitions. The rainbow, the apparition of the few, pure, fundamental, archetypal colours, is the bridge from dappled, multicoloured appearances to the white splendour that unifies all colours and reveals their essence of sheer light:

> Life, like a dome of many-coloured glass,
> Stains the white radiance of Eternity.

All the various points that have been made are beautifully touched on in a poem by Sen-Yo-Rikyu, the Japanese sixteenth-century master of the tea ceremony, a rite in which true attention is brought to bear on what things – the chair, the table, the tea-pot, the cups – actually are:

> The tea ceremony
> is only heating
> the water,
> preparing the tea, and drinking it.

Being as such, beyond all attributes, is symbolised by the tea ceremony, so:

> Make the tea ceremony descend into the heart
> No longer seeing with the eyes,
> No longer listening with the ears.

This is the first phase – abstraction and concentration. Next comes the awareness of archetypal numbers:

> The practice consists in:
> Starting from one, reaching ten,
> Knowing how to come back from ten to one, the origin.

In the inner alchemy whereby the body is separated from the soul, and the soul from the spirit, it is with the isolation of the soul that the archetypes come to the fore. In green alchemy the solid residue of the plants was baked until it turned into a snow-white salt – the pure body of the plant. The liquid mass was distilled until the pungent soul of the plant – its volatile oils – was extracted. The liquid was left to ferment and the result was the spirit of the plant – its eau-de-vie or water of life, its fiery ether, or celestial essence. It was then possible to prepare the 'stone' of the plant. On the white salt the purified soul, preserved in the pure spirit, fell drop by drop, until the three parts coalesced into a stone, in which the life-enhancing properties of the plant were concentrated in such a way that they emanated from it and projected onto other bodies. The same applies to the transformation of men 'into live stones'.

The separation from the psyche and spirit relieves the body of all undue pressures. As a rule the soul unloads her burdens onto her body. She plucks its tissues like chords, giving vent to her passions. Once the body is unyoked, an even flow of energy heals its cramped, shivering organs. The released body reaps all the benefits of healing, dreamless sleep; it is purified and made soulless, just as the plant's salts are calcinated and made colourless.

For her part, the soul, the subtle body wrought by emotions and thoughts, which is ordinarily interfused with the gross body, is wrenched out of it like the aromatic oily part out of the pulp of the plant in the still, and becomes like an effusive aroma, an almost boundlessly elastic field of mesmeric influences, of suggestibility and faith, of imagination. Rumî wrote that spiritually the phantasising soul is nought, but in respect to the ordinary, material world she is everything: men's pride and shame, peace and war, all spring from phantasies (and 'the phantasies that ensnare the saints are the reflection of the moon-faced ones in the garden of God'). As iron filings cluster around magnetic fields, so do souls released from bodily sensations gather round archetypes. In *Ideas of Good and Evil* Yeats explained that all sounds, colours and forms, either because so preordained or because of long association, evoke indefinable yet precise emotions, or rather 'certain disembodied powers, whose footsteps on our hearts we call emotions'.

The distilled soul floats around such naked 'powers', archetypes, darkly drawn to one or to the other, until, free as she is of the gross body, she is buoyed up, finds a safe orbit. This she does delicately groping, not following rules and laws, but in a blind flight, at the end of which she feels centred, achieves a wordless, dreamlike realisation of her destiny. The body caused rigidity, because the soul was led to identify with it, but now she is resilient, pliable, open to slight hints, rare forewarnings, capable of identifying with the soul of all things. Especially that of animals, each species of which embodies an archetype. Shamans learnt the art of entering the world of animals by patiently acquiring their rhythms, imitating the pitch of their voices. A shamanic soul becomes a world-soul. Children and madmen feel the need for this. In Webster's *Duchess of Malfi* the chorus of madmen is an impeccable song of initiation, ranging through the impersonations of all animal-archetypes, to the archetype of archetypes, which in so many Traditions is vehicled precisely by the voice of the swan:

O let us howl, some heavy note,
some deadly-dogged howl,
sounding, as from the threatening throat
of beasts, and fatal fowl.

As Ravens, Screech-owls, Bulls and Bears,
we'll bell, and bawl our parts,
till irksome noise have cloy'd your ears,
and corasiv'd your hearts.
At last when as our quire wants breath
our bodies being blest,
we'll sing like Swans, to welcome death
and die in love and rest.

There is a passage in Hawthorne's *Marble Faun* in which the 'faun', a youth whose soul communes with nature, is shown in the act of expanding his sensitivity, shaman-like, by means of 'a charm – a voice, a murmur, a kind of chant . . . a sort of modulated breath, wild, rude, yet harmonious . . . setting his wordless song to no other or more definite tune than the play of his own pulses . . . of a murmurous character, soft, attractive, persuasive, friendly'. When the murmur is sweet, it is greeted by flutters of wings; when it sours, it is answered by the crawl and shudder of dark forms on the ground – a masterful description of the operations of a disembodied inspired soul. The divining-rod, the painter's brush, the shaman's drumstick, the tranced warrior's sword are swayed by impulses, rhythms that emanate directly from the archetypes. That are in fact the archetypes. Then the body is like a limp, perfect puppet, while the soul glides over the numerous seas of the archetypal world.

10 Realising archetypes through synonymisation

Archetypes are not to be defined and counted, because they lie too deep for words. In the process of definition their ineffable essence is lost. But a list of possible synonyms of 'archetype' can help one realise the meaning without congealing it into a formula.

Seal

Supreme authority is vested in a certifying seal.

Only when stamped by the seal-bearer does a document start to exist. The seal-bearer is the Knower, the active intellect; his various seals, each with its particular scope, represent the archetypes, the Knowing; the papers that bear the stamp are the Known.

The seal-bearer also stands for metaphysical experience, which is reflected in the seals, the archetypes, reflected in their turn by the documents, the concrete things whose force lies in the seal they bear.

One can expand these similes into stories – stories of seals exchanged or stolen or forged or rescued; eventually of seal-rings, and of the fights to gain possession of them.

Name

Children are well aware that the thing named depends on its name. Poets know that you cannot be particular enough about naming a cat. Naming means discovering the controlling archetype. The tremendous importance of naming, for instance among American Indians, does not mean that you have to be stuffy and solemn about it. Naming songs are often funny.

There is a Cree naming song collected by Howard Norman which illustrates superbly a delicate, whimsical, exemplary search for the archetype of a girl. The name given is 'Tree Old Woman', because

> She stood close to a tree and wrinkled
> her face TIGHT
> and this was her tree-bark face.

She would smooth up however, and say that it was because of a woodpecker that had threatened her. One looked up the tree, there was no woodpecker to be seen.

Next you found the girl bathing in the lake – holding on to reeds, 'her legs floating out behind', and she would look up at you and make a turtle-frog's face. She smoothed up however, and said it was because of a turtle-frog that was after her. This time you were not fooled, you did not look for turtle-frogs. The girl ended up by sitting beside an old, old man, their faces close up against one another.

> And hers began
> to wrinkle up again.

So her name is her destiny in short-hand, the organising pattern of her life.

Name and shape describe a being, and name comes first, reflects the archetype. When something changes, a new name is called for, laying claim to a different archetype. A synonym of name is honour, which is what tethers a man, the charm that controls him.

Naming power is supreme power.

God, the supreme power *is* his name.

This is a difficult but logical metaphysical point. The God's presence in a man is His name – the link to Him. If by mentioning it He becomes present, He is His name. If not, He is practically non-existent.

So things are shadows of their names, since names link them to their archetype.

Priests who knew as much knew also that the essence, the value of a thing, was in its name or fame. Therefore if you transfer its name on a bill or a voucher you need not transport it bodily; so values can be moved around without shifting the valuables. Temples were banks.

Money in Sanskrit is *mudrâ*, which is also a sacred cosmic sign.

Templar priests soon discovered the sequence: first comes the tangible commodity; next its name on a bill proves the possessor's claim to it. The name on the bill is all that is needed to obtain what the named commodity is worth. At this point the commodity need not actually exist. Its probability can be named and credited. Next its possibility is enough; finally, its impossibility. This last, supreme development, takes place when Mephistopheles approaches the Emperor, who is broke, and suggests that he issue imperial bills, offering the underground riches of the Empire for security. Now the security actually ensures that those riches will never be mined, since what they are worth is already available in the form of the bills issued on the security of their name. At the end anybody possessing a name will issue promises of payment which are only worth the promise: the act of naming a value creates the value provided the namer has a name.

At this point there is between men a parting of ways. Only a true metaphysician will find things natural from now on. He alone realises that what has happened is only a transfer of all the *mâyâ*, the delusion of reality – previously concentrated in visible, tangible commodities – to their names, which conforms to nature, since names metaphysically precede nameables, values ontologically come before valuables, and God is His name.

Modern money is all this out in the open. States offer no valuables in exchange for the mere name of value, no concrete object in exchange for the sign of its archetype. Gold and jewels were at least rich, glaring symbols; paper money is a mere token. With the former, *mâyâ* at least takes pains to delude; with the latter she shows herself in her sloven nakedness. The naming in itself and by itself creates value. If the circulation of bank-notes is restricted, their value rises – as the sacrifice of the Godhead creates apparent reality.

The privilege of the mint rested originally with the templar priest. He not only issued tokens of (the Name of) his God – signs of a linkage with the God's power, amulets – but also accepted to stamp the God's symbol as security on tokens of value, creating money. All he had to do next was to restrict or expand its circulation, and value would accrue to him out of thin air: from the Godhead, out of the archetype itself. Things were his for the naming.

What of the rate of exchange between bills from various issuing 'naming powers'?

Who decides that goes one further on the temple priest. The broker deals in the comparative prestige of archetypes, making and unmaking the names of naming powers. Money, it is said, is the honour of a king, his name, but a name depends on the bill-broker who deals in the rumours, whispers, arching brows, glitters of the eye that shift the relative value of names, and *he* makes all the value he needs out of the shifts.

What of tangibles, what of valuables once one has reached the purely archetypal level of big banks? They are no longer temples, but they are all the more purely metaphysical.

You think that reality is not *mâyâ*, that the waking world is above dreamland, you believe that what is is, but a nod from above, from where the sheer names are dealt with, and you see what happens to concrete things, to your precious gold, and to your shining jewels, to your heaps of coffee and loads of wheat. You thought yourself a four-square producer, you were convinced that your labour was something to be honoured; but a nod is enough, and your products are fit for the sewer, your sweating self is everybody's laughing-stock.

Only a metaphysician will find this obvious. Others fall into bleak despair, scream out against those who deal in archetypal shifts, as though there existed a way of stabilising values, of making things stay put with the names they have – locked up for ever by the archetype that now happens to animalise them.

Hobbes noticed that whatever enters an account is subject to names, and that what we call items in bills or in books of account the Romans called names. Metaphysics goes beyond this, teaching that names are the essence of the thing named and not mere counters for reckoning, so who controls the archetypal referents can name commodity what he chooses, and it will be his for the naming. Things are their name for the market; the bill-broker by channelling the archetypal energy of greed one way or the other (through rumour, hints, innuendoes) changes the name, the value, the essence of things.

Apart from metaphysical experience, being is being named. God is his Name.

Imagining image

Not just 'image', because the archetype is productive, imaginative, and no image can stand for it for always and exclusively. The archetype of what may be vaguely, hastily, called 'productive passivity' or 'divine mercy' is imagined forth as Mother, the sign of Cancer, a Hollow Cave, the Deep Waters, the full Moon, Milk. But each of these images may stand for something else. Their archetypal function depends on the tone of the phrase, on the tuning of the general attitude. Coomaraswamy suggested a museum of symbols that might fix the most persistent chains of archetypal associations – for instance the archetype of the hinge or hub of the cosmos should be illustrated by a range of images from suns to solar buttons and stirrups, while to the archetype of the Ascent to Heaven would correspond Jacob's ladders, graded pillars, shamans' notched trees, maypoles, decorated masts, scaled Shiva-lingams, central poles of nomads' tents, Brahmanic sacrificial posts, chains-of-arrows.

Idea or shaping form

The synonym 'idea' should stress the intuitive nature of the apprehension of archetypes, of the need for an archetypal illumination, that cannot be replaced by mere study and accumulations of data. Ideas occur, flash, arise out of nowhere, crop up, visit the mind. They are arrived at, they happen. There is a permanent value in the Platonic simile of light projecting the shadows of ideas.

> Of life and death, of happiness and woe,
> Of all that chequers the phantasmal scene
> That floats before our eyes in wavering light,
> Which gleams but on the darkness of our prison
> Whose chains and massy walls
> We feel, but cannot see,

as Shelley wrote in *Queen Mab*, illustrating the idea of Universal Necessity, round whose columns curl all 'multitudinous shapes'.

Another simile hallowed by poetry is that of archetypes standing by the shore of existence and being reflected in the watery surface of everyday life as 'things'.

'Shaping form' also evokes the forces at work within seeds or drops of semen, shaping the material ingredients into plants or animals. Alchemy detected even in metals a shaping form, working on the model of its specific, ideal metallic perfection.

DNA is the coded record of a shaping force's model, of an idea. The archetype or shaping form is constantly at work directing cells to build, heal and mend the ever-faltering, always-dying body, according to the ideal or archetypal pattern. The archetype is not a mere notion, it is the moulding, healing energy, the living presence of what makes hale, whole and holy – the monad, the engendering gender. When a man is close to his archetype he is daemonic, genial, near to perfection perfected, which consists in the total disappearance of everything which is not the working out of the archetypal model. Perfection in other words is the cessation of all interferences, a quasi-unconscious glide through life, within a plain, manifest destiny.

In imperfect cases the presence of the archetype is disturbed and one may be tempted to believe that life is an aggregate of states of mind and of chemical changes in the body, both of which can be easily manipulated.

The fact that material means can change or kill a living creature is not evidence of its material nature. One can take a man's life with a knife but his essence is not a knife; if the killing is not an act of God it must have a meaning: an archetype. The knife is not the explanation.

Meaning

A thing's meaning is what unifies it, hence the Japanese *shimesu*, 'to signify', is akin to *shimeru*, 'to bind, to sum up, to unite'. The meaning of a thing is its compacting and driving archetype. Things are noticed because they have an invariance, a unity, an archetype behind them in which they participate, which they imitate, to use Plato's simile. Shelley's address to Mont Blanc ends with the question:

> And what were thou, and earth, and stars, and sea,
> if to the human mind's imaginings
> Silence and Solitude were vacancy?

The archetype decides what a thing is. The same flesh is alluring in the alcove, where it emanates the symbolic energy of Two-in-One, of Symmetry, but not in the hospital ward, where it ceases to radiate those symbols, and becomes attuned to other ideas, such as that of silent, patient archetypes laboriously moulding matter.

It is the meaning of a thing that we see, the categories that frame it. The Indo-European *mein* – from which 'meaning' stems – meant not only 'indite', 'define', but implied an involvement, and in Celtic languages gave rise to words for lust and will.

Archetypes are unifying patterns, frames of reference laden with psychic energy – meanings.

Meditation is the extraction of meaning from things, and this can be a slow, shuddering process. Rarely has it been described as faithfully as in Wordsworth's famous lines in *The Prelude*:

> After I had seen
> That spectacle, for many days my brain
> Work'd with a dim and undetermin'd sense
> Of unknown modes of being. No familiar shapes
> Remained, no pleasant images of trees,
> Of sea, or sky, no colours of green fields,
> But huge and mighty forms that do not live
> Like living man, mov'd slowly through my mind
> By day and were a trouble to my dreams.

The extraction of the archetypes requires first working with a dim and undetermined sense of an unknown lurking 'presence'. Tree Old Woman's name was arrived at precisely by working in the dusk, tentatively – though without the least hint of weirdness.

Archetypes are something alive, more alive than living creatures, because they are life-giving, meaning-giving. The mind alone cannot apprehend them, and they can shatter a heart of stone, melt a heart of ice, trample a heart of flesh. They are, according to Jung's metaphor, psychic magnetic fields. Material bodies are mere conductors of their energy, which is the force of symbolisation.

Every human body is a conductor with a peculiar magnetic field of its own, its psyche. The approach of a stronger field of energy can be devastating; the psyche is necessarily moved and changed, sometimes it ceases to exist under the impact.

11 Realising archetypes through similitudes

Clouds

Archetypes hover over a psyche like clouds above a landscape. When the psyche is peaceful, clouds will show forth the laws of composition and harmony. Chinese painting manuals, like Goethe and Ruskin, insist on the art of enjoying them as they manifest unity in the very changefulness of their shapes. A mind with a strong sense of Oneness is delighted by the sweet interplay of floating mists, as it is by the corresponding interlacing of feelings and thoughts.

Painters place amid the clouds personified archetypes. Poets hear voices drifting through the cloudscape; up in the mists Shelley's Asia calls out to Panthea, asking what beings she sees taking shape among the billows, and Panthea replies:

> A countenance with beckoning smiles: there burns
> An azure fire within its golden locks!
> Another and another: hark! They speak!

The clouds at harvest-time set Hopkins crying:

> . . . what lovely behaviour
> Of silk-sack clouds! has wilder, wilful-wavier
> Meal-drift moulded ever and melted across skies?
> I walk, I lift up, I lift up heart, eyes,
> Down all that glory in the heavens to glean our saviour,
> And eyes, heart, what looks, what lips yet gave you a
> Rapturous love's greeting of realer, of rounder replies?

To the man who has lost contact with unity it will be impossible to catch the unifying, harmonising tone of a cloudscape; he shall construe bleak, lurid scenes in the fogs, he shall behave like an animal unnerved by thunderclaps.

Expanses of water

The eye charmed by rolling vapours is equally attracted to vast expanses of water. Their calm soothes, their shifting instructs, their fury intoxicates. Like clouds, they are a choice metaphor of the intermediary archetypal world. They can convey thither.

The sea looks like one huge, compact liquid mass – but a keen eye, lulled by the alpha-inducing ebb and flood, learns to detect distinct layers, currents wending their way through stiller bodies of water, exactly as the intermediary or psychic world assembles into distinct archetypes. When a storm rages, the masses of water rise and whirl wildly, crushing into one another, as archetypes in a stormy psychic medium collide and form vortexes.

Vortexes

A giddy mind tugged by archetypes resembles a gulf that opposing surges twist and turn into a funnel. Shamans expose themselves on purpose to frightening pressures, contriving to form an inner vortex, making their psyche spin and gather speed until they are transformed into whirlwinds sweeping away all resistance even on their worldly path, but maintaining a void cone round the axis of their verticalised psyche. They thus tumultuously touch illumination and metaphysical experience. Keats's Glaucus cries:

> through some sucking pool I will be hurled
> with rapture the other side of the world.

The vortex also forms a cone of power in the direction of the surrounding world.

In sacred drinking bouts, drug rituals, and bloody Dionysian festivals, this kind of reeling ecstasy was sought while maintaining at the same time perfect self-possession. The unleashed might rocked the soul, but inside the maelstrom there was peace and inflexible determination. Drinking bouts among the Norsemen were compared to riding into battle or being hanged – one had to maintain control at the core of the fury, absorbing the storm and turning it in the desired direction. The Norse *Havamal* gives instructions:

> When you drink ale   assume the power of earth!
> Because earth sucks up ale   like fire contagion.

All this pertains to the Dionysian archetype, in which outward savagery and inward serenity can coexist. Dionysus is a warrior who conquers India, propelled through the country like a whirlwind, but with his sweet smile intact, his soul at peaceful rest. Alexander the Great pretended to imitate him, even to mad drinking bouts and murder. The same archetype, exempt from all savagery, spins the dance of the Hours in Shelley's *Prometheus Unbound*:

> We whirl, singing loud, round the gathering sphere,
> Till the trees, and the beasts, and the clouds appear
> from its chaos made calm by love, not fear.

When this archetype looms supreme over the world, the origin of everything is conceived as a churning of the primeval ocean.

The myth recounts that at the beginning of beginnings all was an ocean of subtle matter. In India it was called an ocean of milk, in which fire, water and earth; butter, whey and curd; spirit, soul and body; were one. In the ocean, it is sometimes added, there floated a golden womb, and a womb is mercy, active passivity incarnate.

Demons and gods churn the Ocean of Oneness and the hurricane divides the elements. Multiplicity results. Among peoples to whom the dairy is a temple, making cheese is a celebration of cosmogony.

Rituals of intoxication with the churning in the background make man into the cosmos by turning him into a drunken vortex. The same end is achieved in the mode of quietude by meditating on the potter's wheel, the lathe, the spindle, the axle. Spires soaring heavenward, or plunging downward, all carry the same archetypal message; life itself is a spiral uncoiling from seed to tree and back, from egg to bird and back, from the instant of revelation to the consequent cycle of history and back. It is seen in the pit that from the lips of the womb rises to the source of life, as in the vice-like tendrils of vines. It is heard in the mounting moan and shriek, in the rising invocation, in the hum of the orbiting bull-roarer, in tensing, quickening drumbeats. In Yoga the imagination is trained to see seven centres or lotuses of power in the body, from where the tail might hang and be flourished up to where the skull was open and pulsating at birth. The lotuses next become *chakras*, rotating turbines. Caught in their helixes the two balanced – and therefore normally unsensed – forces, the two main currents of energy, past and future, sun and moon, give and take, now twist and turn, are thrust one against the other, and start circling, spinning madly. The serpentine power coiled up near the tail now darts up through the rings, hurtling beyond the opposition of conscious and unconscious into total deliverance.

Blake's famous summarising verses teach an exercise of the imagination that can lead to this experience – which Yoga also commends:

> Let the human Organs be kept in their perfect Integrity,
> At will contracting into Worms or Expanding into Gods.

Blake suggests we become one with the weeping clod in the ploughed furrow, contracting, and that we then rise upon the chariots of the morning, expanding. All around us the whole universe will appear like a host of contracting and expanding vortices, of *chakras*:

> The nature of infinity is this: That everything has its
> Vortex.
>
> Thus is the heaven a vortex pass'd already and the earth
> A vortex not yet pass'd by the traveller thro' Eternity.

Blake alone specifically depicted the world of archetypes or vortexes, all material props removed, in the purity of visionary geography as revealed by a full identification with the Dionysian archetype.

12 How many archetypes there are

The difficulty in counting archetypes lies in the fact that, being too deep for words, they cannot and must not be whittled down to definitions.

Among certain peoples for certain periods a list of archetypes was, however, drawn up. It hung on the main figures observed in the skies or on other stable sets. It was used for ordering the world and the calendar, for organising the State, for creating corresponding psychotherapeutic pantheon-mandalas, and for divination; the *I Ching* and geomancy survive. Alphabets were originally lists of archetypes, ours starting from Alpha, the Bull of sacrifice, and Beta, the temple and sacrificial bowl or grail.

Once a set of archetypes has been thought out, its persistence is bewildering. From deep down in the pit of the past rose the archetypal figures that beckoned from the walls of Christian churches, and in their novel disguise they seemed to have both staying power and a fierce will to oust all others systems; and yet when, after their long and strict domination, it happened that Freud made a few discoveries and needed moulds for them, the best he could find available were the old Greek stock characters, Oedipus, Narcissus, Orestes.

An archetypal system worthy of its name, such as we still find among the Ewe or the Dogons, assigns to each archetype, visualised as a God, a peculiar signifier or symbol on each level of being. Thus is created a network or grid connecting a corresponding particular number and geometrical figure, a rhythm, a timbre and a note, a musical instrument, a utensil and a weapon, a stone and a metal, a herb and an animal, a section of the year and a portion of space, a colour, an odour and a taste, a part of the body and a human character, a star.

But from an archetypal system something must always be left out, a part must always fade off into a haze, data at a certain point must get mixed up, so that nobody will ever be tempted to feed them to a computer. The system is not to be learned by rote. As in painting, the manner of the master must be absorbed, the rest left to inspiration; the symbolisation of archetypes is a way of life, to be experienced in a state of intoxication and rapture. Clear-cut yes-or-nos, this-or-thats, will not work on the archetypal level. Archetypes rotate all the time; they are not to be manipulated. As with the unconscious, in dealing with them, one must give up negation, dyadic thinking. Mesmerisers know that negative commands do not work in hypnosis. Exorcists use only positive injunctions. Languages actually have no exclusively and originally negative particles. *Ne* in Indo-European is an ironically stressed emphatic particle. Most insults are sarcastic praise, as the old 'to horn', in the sense of 'cuckold'. Words in ancient languages denote a complex, a direction, and not one definite thing or other. The Italic goddess Mefis was everything one felt near sulphurous, mefitic exhalations, even aversion to them – so she was also she-who-averted-stenches. In English this persists in an adjective like 'apparent', which can mean both 'manifest' and 'seeming'.

Such all-comprising words conform to archetypal reality. Also certain social arrangements and institutions show an archetypal sense of reality, especially in subtle South Seas societies, where all is centred round charisma, *mana*. This power, comparable to that of a nearing archetype, enables the possessor to impose taboos, but it is by infringing taboos that he displays and strengthens his *mana*. This holds good with society in general, but there exists a fraternity, the Arioi, who specialise in the archetypal. They are clowns who recount, sing and dance the myths; they conduct sacrifices, give sexual shows, kill their offspring and ignore taboos, but act as police, obliging others to observe them. They alone advance in their ranks on the basis of merit, disregarding *mana*. They ended by being identified with the archetypes – the unconscionable, the unrestrained and elusive gods they represented on the stage, whose taboos they enforced and whose sacrifices they celebrated.

Access to the archetypal in most societies is granted by sacrifice, which is a paradox and a subversion. The sacrificer's cry is 'I so love you that I must kill you'. Life is inaugurated by a scream of horror, and all action is a violation of purity, all speech a desecration of inward truth; all signifiers are victims of meaning, all encounters are a menace, all incarnations a sin. On the other hand sacrifice also signifies that gain springs from loss, energy from exertion. Potlatches increase wealth by squandering. So sacrifice seems the proper response to life.

Mothers and lovers stroke and claw, hug and bite in their overflow of archetypal intensity; they whisper 'I'll eat you', and mean it.

Juridical systems are always mixing up punishment and reward – being sent to the vanguard is an honour for a soldier, and yet it is where the worst criminals are sentenced to serve.

Among Pueblos whipping is inflicted on miscreants and is

thought to bring good luck and heal rheumatism. In Germany on Holy Innocents' Day and for the New Year boys and girls took turns in happily caning one another – and to go scot free from Easter smacks was a disgrace.

Kingship and crime both 'make sacred' and are both a case for 'handing over to a god', so kings were ritually murdered or flogged.

A keen eye for the archetypal level – which stands out fully revealed in the incongruous aspects of society – teaches us to twist aspersions into praise, as was done with *les gueux*, the 'contemptibles', the 'desert rats'. Nice comes from nescient, and vice versa silly meant happy, artificial artistic, cretin Christian.

What a term actually means depends on its relationship with the archetypes, and this can be inferred from the general context, from the pervading tone.

It matters little whether you praise or condemn, or under what heading you place a thing. The archetypal level takes its revenge on those who think they can ignore it and chain things to one meaning.

When there is a change of archetypal influences afoot, it matters little whether one fights for or against it; novelties will thrive on insult and on praise alike. Whether you persecute or you favour a sect on the make, you are paying it honour – making a name for it.

If you want a fad to stick, get somebody to run it down. Only on controversy will it thrive.

Only a fine sense of pitch can tell what is actually intended when something is extolled or derided. Look at snapshots of people mourning – they seem to be laughing, and vice versa at festivals.

It needs an ear for shading, a sense of the archetypal shifts, to know what is actually going on. Keats's Lamia speaks of how:

> To unperplex bliss from its neighbour pain,
> Define their pettish limits, and estrange
> Their points of contact, and swift counterchange;
> Intrigue with the specious chaos, and dispart
> Its most ambiguous atoms with sure art.

When an archetype holds something in its clutches, it makes it obsessive, compacts it, causing it to appear enigmatic, self-existent: comprising good and bad, ego and id, honour and disgrace.

The poet therefore uses signifiers of archetypes rather than binary – good versus bad – notation.

In general, heavily laden and ambiguous enigmas are used in order to penetrate the outer layer of oneself or of others. Stressed signifiers in a particular context will send a current of symbolising energy to unconscious strata.

When not by habit, but unexpectedly, all of sudden a man feels impelled to call a small girl 'you little rabbit', a complicated criss-cross of messages is flashed. 'Rabbit' in due context lights up all that in a man's unconscious memory may correspond to what in history have been the cult of the rabbit in the moon, the worship of the rabbit-like swift planet Venus, the springtime watching of rabbit dances, and rabbit-totem dances. The same circuit of signifiers is activated which in past times made of the rabbit a symbol of Lord Buddha, made it taboo as food among Celts and Jews, made a trickster of it in Mexico, and makes American boys nudge and whisper 'she screws like a bunny'.

A man feels strangely, unavowably moved – 'you little rabbit' conveys what he might not like to look into too closely, and what would anyway defy definition, though one may surmise that it has something to do with Pan, who was wrapped up by his mother in a soft rabbit's skin.

There are a few such persistent signifiers which all down a long line of generations seem capable of electrifying souls, of generating a direct contact with an archetype. It seems that the image of a lush meadow can trigger a telling response in most minds, and a psychiatric method has been accordingly developed.

Disturbed minds usually find difficulty in visualising and meditating on such a meadow. It evokes the archetype of surrender and inner peace. In fables it is the land of the blissful, where years contract to seconds, or vice versa – Elysium. A diseased psyche cannot stand the idea of a total renewal. The visualisation of a meadow is consequently impaired – the grass will appear withered, the ground broken with stumps.

Emphasis on such a symbol sensitises something deep in the psyche, which escapes conscious awareness. When a meadow is meditated on in a dreamlike state, free-floating symbolic energies are activated, which may hamper the visualisation. They are the very same energies which in dreams would eventually project images of desolate, waste meadowland.

13 What archetypes do to man

An archetype is what can permanently order objects into sets, gather together emotions, and direct thoughts.

Contact with an archetype cannot be revealed in the language of everyday experience; it requires exclamatory and idiomatic expressions; it is always attended by some measure of entrancement. But a sense of archetypes can also dawn on ordinary minds, caught in the web of manifold, benumbing appearances. To these minds the encounter will be a startling, fearsome reversal of their stiff, fragile, thoughtless, clumsy habits and persuasions, of their previous unthinking, unstable archetypal balance. Such minds may blunder into archetypes as they grope their way in the maze of material causes. Or a slighted archetype may grip them all of a sudden: love may clench them when they are playing the wanton; fury seize them on a trifling occasion; despair overcome them precisely when status is ensured, duty performed, affection secured. They may think they have settled all a nation's problems, satisfied its needs, furthered its interests – and somebody turns up reversing archetypes: 'Ask not what your country can do for you, but what you can do for your country,' and the too down-to-earth, too sensible, too healthy, too self-seeking voters will become sacrifice-eager, danger-courting, entranced dreamers. Many times it is in sleep, or with strange slips, unintended acts, that neglected archetypes visit their first slight punishments on one who has dared ignore them. Many then exclaim with Hamlet:

> O God! I could be bounded in a nut-shell, and count myself a king of infinite space; were it not that I have bad dreams.

In society at large, a neglect of archetypes will bring about the appearance of strange and estranged minorities on far-out, unpleasant fringes. The warning is sounded; if it go unheeded, the brunt will be paralysing, the archetype will carry its victims off in a swoon.

Man needs axioms for his thinking, food for his body, trance for his psyche. Trance means going beyond (*trans ire*) into the archetypal world. When one grazes it, at shows or in dalliance, it gives a mild thrill; but that is not enough, only panic will do. It is man's lot to lose himself periodically in the forest of archetypes. This happens in dreams, which reveal the actual archetypal purport of everyday existence. In dreams one sees the nonsensical farce of one's involvement in appearances, identification with semblances, entanglement with reminiscences, because, once sleep has sent the psyche adrift, forms and images are arranged according to their archetypal import alone. So one comes up against what is inescapable. One is exposed to it naked, and fearing, or wondering. But dreaming is not enough. Men cannot survive without periodically disappearing, fully awake, into an archetype. They need to feel carried away in broad daylight by the impending archetype. They feel a call from the Primordial Dyad or Symmetry, and fall to mating; they want to be dazzled by the Emergence-of-the-Unit-of-Measure, and rush to gamble; they are attracted into the varying significance that brawling, drinking, dancing, banqueting and haranguing can assume. Sensible social arrangements in certain groups provide for periodic sessions of spirit possession, which afford a totally satisfying surrender to the needed archetype. Originally, dances so increased their tempo, and singing grew so hoarse, that possession followed – as among Vedda shamans in Sri Lanka. Also, at Yaqui and Taosian festivals the capers and the leaps result in trances. Originally, among South American shamans, smoking brought them to the point of swooning and hallucination.

An archetype is generally acted out in the form of a recital. Most people have a peculiar mythic event, a dream sequence that they feel compelled to go through over and over again in a state of slight intoxication, like children absorbed in their game. The most telling and graphic rendition of this truth can be found in Genêt's plays. His Universal Brothel is the archetypal social institution, where everybody's personal arch-dream is catered to.

Most people are struck by an archetype – by its mythical incarnation in an event – at least once in their lifetime, and after that all they can do is circle round and round it. They are literally enchanted, bewitched, doomed to eternal circumambulation, and it is incredibly difficult to find the right disenchanting chant for them. Whatever happens is either crammed into the general picture of their obsession or is allowed to flit past unheeded.

It is not only in Victorian novels that an existence full of apparent change and adventure may hinge on the childhood or adolescent memory of a smart or of a slight, or of a mere snub, or of some puerile disappointment or attraction or commitment. The squaring of the imaginary account, the paying off of the stale score, is the very gist of such lives, and yet the Victorian writer knew that he had the reader safely on the stubborn hero's side. It is considered natural that the stunted soul shall roam the globe, engage in the wildest enterprises, and then come back to some funny native village to call quits. 'Changing place changes stars' runs a Jewish saying, but it falls on deaf ears with people whose stunned psyches, wherever the body may be, remain glued to the spot of their encounter with the archetype. The soul has been transformed into a pillar of salt.

When the primal paralysing scene is buried away in early infancy, and not even remembered, the victim is like the man in the experiment Bernheim was fond of showing his pupils, the youthful Freud among them. The man was put under hypnosis and told to carry out some silly action later on. When the time came, he did what he had been ordered, with a puzzled air, but finding some rational excuse to cover up his behaviour. An archetypal encounter has implanted such an order in most people, and they waste away their lives, obeying as best they may and with the most strained justifications. Sometimes they inherit the pattern from their parents. They are never awakened, not even to be crippled and mesmerised.

The Ideal Universal Brothel provides a straight man to feed each client his lines in his particular farce. The official who has slipped back into his school uniform will get his spanking; the colonel who has donned priestly vestments will hear the desired confession. If some such Brothel is not providing an outlet, the archetype will assert itself anyway; mouthings, grimaces, nervous tics will devastate the deprived one's face. They cannot be stopped: whatever the circumstances, he must go on frantically playing his part over and over in the archetypal mythic scene in which those movements are required. Stutters, compulsions, repetitions, the trite mistakes made over and over again, expletives, redundancies in general are signs that the person, whatever the cost, is trying to act out the archetypal dream, his or her curse.

As Hopkins phrased it:

> Self-yeast of spirit a dull dough sours. I see
> The lost are like this, and their scourge to be
> As I am mine, their sweating selves . . .

Redundancy is the key that locks them in, and could eventually also unlock them.

What a man feels compelled pointlessly to voice gives his game away. All oath taking, swearing, all the mad mythology of invectives, all the moronic sexual metaphors are avowals of obsessions. With such victims of mythic compulsions, whether they are honest, law-abiding zombies or reasonably neurotic patients, it has been suggested that the cure might be for them to repeat untiringly the questions: 'Who am I? What *is* I?' This might lead to the realisation that personal identity is a delusion, that one is not one but many, until at last non-personal awareness, a witnessing anonymous centre, is firmly established: a non-personal identity which is cosmic, sheer being.

If this is not achieved, what difference does it make that it is you or somebody else, with another name, that goes through your body's mechanical set of motions? They are the result of social myths, of conditionings you have never even inquired about. You or somebody else – it makes no difference whatever.

To gain this point of view, one should pay a visit to Genêt's Brothel, which Blake styled 'Halls of Los':

> All things acted on Earth are seen in the bright Sculptures of
> Los's Halls and every Age renews its powers from these Works,
> With every pathetic story possible to happen from Hate or

> Wayward Love and every sorrow and distress is carved here,
> Every affinity of Parents, Marriages and Friendships are here
> In all their various combinations wrought with wondrous Art.

The same key can unlock; let a man shed his redundancies and he will be a buoy in the sea of archetypes. He will view the Halls of Los detachedly; the Universal Brothel will appear to him a collection of curios.

The temporary satisfaction he got out of his little act in this or that chamber of the Universal Brothel was a tame affair by comparison – nothing but a temporary release from pressure, the daily dose of the addict, while a realisation of the game of archetypes behind it all will confer a sense of release, of peace and ecstasy only inferior to the full peace and bliss of unity, to the realisation of cosmic Oneness.

A novel of Ouspensky tells the story of a man who is expelled from school, loses an inheritance, a job, a fiancée, and begs a magician for help. The magician consents to give him a new lease on life and projects him backward in time, to his earlier years. The man makes the same mistakes, one by one, all over again – even though he now knows each time what the outcome will be. The old, unchanging compulsion is irresistible, so he finds himself back in the magician's presence. He finally discovers that the only answer is to shed his silly self. He looks at the cats in a Moscow lane and realises the meaning of the impersonal here-and-now.

The average human being clings madly to the rags of his 'personality'; in them he drapes himself for the monotonous, tiresome, dreary performance of the one archetypal myth which is his personal equation. If ever he realised the here-and-now, he would also see the myth as if from outside himself; then he would heave a deep sigh of relief, like Sinbad after having shaken the mean old man off his shoulders. He would then be granted the realisation of what archetypes are – what Keats called a fellowship with essences, a 'sort of oneness' that brings freedom and renewal. But such an enthralment, Keats adds, is 'self-destroying'; it is barred to the multitudes who refuse to let go of their selves.

Yet everybody knows about archetypes. There isn't a village

where you are not reminded of them, at least comically, by statues, by decorations, by buildings designed not to provide shelter but to symbolise. You cannot handle a banknote without being stared at by them: they hang on walls, dangle on chests, are worn on fingers. Everybody serves archetypes, but only a few understand what they are. A shaman once risked his life to become all archetypes – to impersonate them, not as tranced and possessed, unconscious devotees might, but as an actor glowingly committed though fully aware of the performance. This enabled him to *use* archetypes instead of remaining their plaything. He became the lawgiver, and was no longer a law-abiding serf or a tormented law-breaker.

Since the realisation of the nature of archetypes is a rare feat, naming them presents the biggest problem in language. How can their necessarily unconscious, submerged part be identified? It should be done through poetry. Or by a sacred dumbshow dancer – moving, say, his hand in circles around his heart and showing all things issuing thence. Some think that the naming should be spiced with suffering, enhanced by powerful hallucination. Certainly it cannot be done without emotion, but the emotion must be symbolically transposed and clarified; it should become an evocation through symbol, as Yeats explained in *Dramatis Personae*. All emotions are event-raising evocations. Do not fierce haters seem to generate violence outside their control? Thanks to symbols, emotions are channelled. A meditation on sunlight creates what the sun symbolises; 'an emotion produces a symbol – sensual emotion dreams of water, for instance, just as a symbol produces emotion'. The assumption follows that an archetype is impending when a symbol and an emotion coalesce. Meditation on symbols can teach one to sense the plexuses.

III *Archetypal Politics*

14 Archetypes in politics. The archetype of Rome

Grasping the role of archetypal evocations in politics is a helpful exercise – noticing how each generation seems to get stuck in some primal political scene, after which it is boxed in, incapable of renewed attention. The categories within which events are apprehended seem to have been fixed once and for all by the generations who went through the successive European wars or revolutions. Those generations were crippled psychically, never outgrowing their single frame of reference: the pattern of alliances, the stock characterisations. Whatever may happen has to be referred back to the primal scene. The game must never change. Practical statesmen well know that nothing stays put, but they must condescend to the old linguistic identifications to get through with business.

These stultifying games are side-acts in a vaster show, in which nations are engaged for centuries at a stretch, after some great myth-maker has set a scenario, called down one or two archetypes, which thenceforth will blind men to all the remaining components of life – to the point of political colour blindness, fanaticism. To the redundancies in gestures, the expletives in language, the tics that testify to the private mythical acts interminably rehearsed, there exist corresponding analogous political quirks. In fact it is easier for a man to disengage from his private obsessions than to see through the painted veil of political fables, especially when these are presented as history or as general interest. The interest is not of the generality as such, but of its unifying myth. History would not cohere if mythical trends were not read into it.

The extent of political delusions can be gauged by how easily, in political disputations, people surrender to phrases such as 'If everybody thought and/or did as you do . . .', whose validity should rest on sober evidence that the culprit's thoughts or deeds carry substantial weight in general affairs. When reasoning is blurred to the extent that such a phrase is taken seriously, it is a sign that an archetype is inflating the ego.

The archetypes that rule political life change slowly along the millennia. It is of paramount importance to realise this if one is to understand the workings of archetypes in general.

European history is a fugue built on a handful of mythical themes. It all started with the terrific story of the founding of Rome, a name sometimes interpreted as Love, *Amor* in reverse. On a vestal virgin Mars sires the twins Romulus and Remus. They are abandoned in a trough on the Tiber and end up under a fig tree, where a she-wolf suckles them and a woodpecker feeds them, perhaps with the sap of the tree. A shepherd and his wife, Faustus and Acca Larentia, act as foster parents to the two, who become warriors and avenge their dead mother. (In some versions, all woes are due to a wicked uncle, often the main personage in matriarchal societies.) The warrior twins found a city on the hills surrounding the fig tree, but omens decree that Romulus shall be the true founder. Remus, from the Aventine, spots six vultures, but Romulus later descries twelve from the Palatine and thus wins the contest. He proceeds to plough the circuit of Rome and when Remus oversteps it he kills him for the sacrilege. The city becomes a sanctuary for the stragglers of the region, and oRmulus turns them into a disciplined fighting force. The most experienced of them he appoints to a senate. Then he disappears, ascending to heaven.

Bands of nomad warrior youths of a Romulian kind were known in ancient Persia. On their banner a dragon stood out against a black background. They practised, according to Wikander, a form of ritual intercourse with prostitute-priestesses and sought to maintain themselves in a state of rabid intoxication, drinking *haoma* and identifying themselves with the dragon-slayer. They were called 'two-footed wolves'. They differed from the Romulian squads because of their knightly interest in the protection of maidens. Otherwise, points of contact with the archaic Persian institution can be found at all points of the Romulian myth. The fig tree was sacred to Venus and Dionysus the intoxicator; fig juice fermented could replace *haoma*. There were fraternities devoted to fig secrets. 'Sycophants' were divulgers ('figs' in Greek are *sykòi*) of fig lore, which was linked with crime, wolves, and ritual lewdness. In Greece, criminals expelled from towns wore necklaces of figs. Roman matrons, with their maids, celebrated the fig festival of Juno, in which they touched with fig twigs – like Tantric devotees with lingams – men's sex organs and their own.

Among Roman youths there was the fraternity of wolves (*luperci*). Cicero talks about wolfish brothers who enact something belonging to earlier, less humane times. At their festival, which fell in February, they killed a goat, touched their foreheads with its blood, as if consigning themselves to death, and then wiped it off with wool (*februm*). After this they ran naked (the Persian counterparts made a point of fighting nude), plying women with freshly cut strips of the hairy goat's hide. They rounded the Palatine, their centre being the she-wolf's den (*lupercal*). The she-wolf of the legend had lost her cubs (*lup* in Etruscan means death). The she-wolf demon in Babylon was death, especially that of sucklings. It is death's milk the twins Romulus and Remus drank; they belonged to the world of devouring demons. But *lupa* in Latin also means a prostitute. Acca Larentia, the twins' foster mother, is described as a loose woman in certain versions, and her name connects her with the dead (*lares*). All this points to a roaming guild of fig-tree priestesses devoted to cults of death and sex. The leaders of woodpeckers' guilds in Humbria imitated the knocks of the bird's beak against the bark of the tree with a hammer of fecundity. The sap was fermented.

Twins have appeared horrifying to many tribes all over the world, so they were often, at least one of them, put to death. They were discord and doubt (*dubium*, dual being) incarnate. Everything sinister is present in the Romulian tale: wolfishness, lewdness, lawlessness, the marshalling of the riffraff, and at the same time judicial murder, the strictest of law enforcements. The number of

Romulus, since he is added to Larentia's family of twelve, is thirteen. He appears to be the equivalent of the English countryside Tommy with his Bess, a man in disguise – a springtime lightning god. He founds his city on 21 April 754 BC. He resembles Cain, the founder of cities, who became untouchable thanks to murder and bore a bloody sign on his forehead like a *lupercus*.

The tale serves many good mythic turns. All lively boys dream that they are bastards of a high-ranking kind. Everything that lives on the fringe of society is alluring; the story holds the unchanging appeal of cowboy, pirate, and criminal stories, with dark hints at more and worse. It represents society in the raw, at its criminal inception, untouched by family romance, simplified by main force, wary about omens, and shorn of pity. It is a barracks myth, the consecration of the ruthless bully who, however roughly, provides for his comrades. The deities are Mars, and in the background wild Venus, and Vulcan – connected with the vestals. Mars will further shower his blessings by dropping his shields on the Capitol. They signify protection; when struck, they make a warlike din; they catch the sun's reflection and blind whoever dares raise his head in front of them. Their concavity serves as a stretcher; on their convex side, leaders are carried in triumph.

Under such a thirteenish and dual archetype of dire manly comradeship nobody will dare show anything but sternness, punctiliousness, curtness, level-headedness, endurance, reliance on ritual and signs, rough solidarity.

The myth of Romulus provided a strong archetypal girdle for the city – which had, however, something less sinister to fall back on: the myth of the Pythagorean king Numa, the sage who sought inspiration from a nymph. But this story always took a back seat. Rome was essentially Romulian.

Barracks may look strong, but they fall prey to rivalries and internal coups. Comradeship works both ways: it can make command easy or it can favour mutiny. Either a good impersonator of Romulus keeps the rugged mass spellbound with a display of all the ingredients of the myth or the element of equality in comradeship comes to the fore and the mythical energy is channelled into comitial rule. At the end of the Republic, the myth was fraying. Whoever among the Romulian impersonators got deepest into debt with the bankers was bound to become the chief, but to stay on he needed a new myth, besides and above the old soldierly one.

If Antony, who identified with Dionysus, had prevailed, the imperial myth would have been that of the double crown of the land of the Nile, a most time-hallowed story known in Latium well before Rome: the Sun becomes a human ruler with a claim to whatever land is blessed by the rays of his heavenly double. But it was Augustus who carried the day. He started his archetypal manoeuvring by becoming supreme pontiff. When he took over he had the myth all squared out, and Virgil, the most melodious of poets, turned it into verse for him. He, like Romulus, was descended from Aeneas, the Trojan prince. He went back even to before Romulus. He identified his destiny with that of Troy, the great defeated city of the Mediterranean world. Since Greece was under the Roman yoke, accounts were neatly settled. Troy had been avenged by her sons. They had endured through the centuries because they were one with Venus, Mars's Shakti, who could be wolfish and simple but was essentially gentle and courtly. The Imperial Father myth took precedence over the soldierly myth; it offered a more settled yin–yang balance. It also enjoyed the advantage of incorporating the theme of 'the return of the repressed' – a defeated race warily preparing its comeback through the ages, with its arcana, its esoteric political secrets passed patiently on from father to son, along with the faith in the gods, who would never forsake their trusting devotees. The world was Rome's because of the primal right of revenge and because of the manifest assistance of Venus (and Mars). Just in case the Egyptian myth might have something to it, Rome was studded with obelisks imported from the shores of the Nile, to bring down into her soil whatever archetypal imperial energy might be had through them.

The West has never shaken off the Augustan myth of empire which took over the powerful 'Roman name', *nomen romanum*. Whatever else the various emperors tried out in the way of archetypes failed to stick. Nero toyed with Persian imports; since Persia had developed an imperial myth as powerful as Egypt's, he sought a consecration by Magi. Other emperors called down various Syrian combinations, but the Romulian-Augustan, Mars-Venus combination held good.

When Christ's disciples changed the psychic atmosphere, the old formula was not discarded; Constantine decided to improve on it, making it dual, as the Egyptian settlement had been. He staged the most dazzling of pageants in AD 330, near Troy – at the opposite end and on the other side of the Straits – and there founded the second Rome, Constantinople, which was actually Rome coming back to the ancient shores, to where the whole story had started. All the magic relics of the Capitol were brought here amid these other Seven Hills, but with them manna from Israel's medicine pouch, since it was felt that Christ was entitled to take over all that magic too. On the top of a column rising in the centre of the city stood a statue of the emperor as the Sun, and rays around his head were made of the nails of the Holy Cross. The new, the second, Rome was Troy, Golgotha, and Capitol all in one.

When the old Rome fell to Odoacer, the barbarian king deposed the last Western emperor, conveniently named Romulus Augustulus, and sent off to the only remaining emperor the insignia of authority. So Rome was one once more. Christianity had reinforced the mythic scenario, and the emperor's old pontifical role was now enlarged; he presided over the ecumenical councils, was called God's 'icon' or 'archetype', like a real pharaoh. His fortune manifested God's Word, according to inscriptions.

But Rome was still there, the original scenario. And its bishops were busy filching slowly and slyly – or so it seemed in Byzantium – the pontifical imperial role. They avoided claiming other, secular powers, preferring to stay emperor-makers, instead of simple emperors. This was one esoteric point they proved they had mastered. The other was the knowledge that written names control the things named, and their Curia specialised in drawing up documents, something as important as the privilege of the mint that nobody dared deny the Roman emperor of the East. (The bezant outlasted even Byzantium; it took a long time before the triumphant Arabs coined money of their own.) When the Roman bishops, by now pontiffs, decided that they felt safer with a territory of their own, all they had to do was draw up a donation for the required domain bearing the signature of Constantine himself. When the Muslim fleet attacked the second Rome, the bishop of the first Rome thought he saw his chance to reject imperial supremacy, but he paid for the mistiming with his life. It was only two and a half centuries later that one of his successors could safely crown Charlemagne the Holy Roman Emperor of the West. The Frankish chief seems to have protested to the very end of his days his ignorance of what the crafty pontiff was up to during the ceremony of Christmas night in the year 800, bestowing on him the secular power but keeping for himself the pontifical authority, the very first that Augustus had secured. Dante was still indignant after four hundred years: how could another emperor be crowned when the lawful one was reigning in Byzantium? The Augustan myth was now alive in a Western version, but with the pontifical authority distinct, claiming the function of *Cakravartin*, he-who-turns-the-wheel-of-destiny, and empire. The Western empire was less stable in regard to myths than was the Roman empire of the East, where the relation between church and emperor was neatly marked out and not, as in the West, wavering between the temptation of a full seizure of power on the part of the pontiff – a temptation that nearly carried away Gregory VII – and the practice of cautiously tipping the balance of power between the emperor and the intermediary bodies, using the spiritual weapons to favour the lower orders if necessary.

Otto was the only emperor who would not wholly remit the pontifical rights he felt were due him, and he had bells dangling from his garments like a biblical pontiff. Emperors did not impinge on pontifical power, but helped those forces that might counter it, such as the doctrines of utter ecclesiastical poverty favoured by the mendicant orders, and even downright heresy. The whole history of the Middle Ages hinges on the various interpretations allowed by the mythical setting that Augustan poetry and statecraft had framed.

Dante thought that the Roman Empire had been patently justified by God when He chose to send His Son on earth at the very beginning of imperial rule, when Rome had just cleared the way for evangelisation by unifying the world, so to speak. Christ was thereby a Roman. The Church should be restricted by a strong imperial hand. This was the way of Byzantium. Dante placed his hopes in the Emperor Henry VII. The emperor also enjoyed the spiritual assistance of the German knightly poet Wolfram von

Eschenbach, who reformulated the myth of the Holy Grail, neatly splicing the old Celtic stories with Persian imperial mythic lore; in the context a ritual of the Holy Grail was envisaged whose main elements were those sections of the Mass that the Roman pontiffs had discarded and Byzantium had preserved.

The imperial side was that of all the great poets of Italy. Petrarch placed *his* hopes in the emperor of his time, Charles VII, and also in the Roman rabble-rouser Rienzi, who seemed about to bring the Roman people back to life as a political entity. Ariosto's hopes rested in Charles V, whom Titian painted as Marcus Aurelius. The last showdown between the emperor and the pontiff took place with the sack of Rome, Lutheran soldiery doing the job. Campanella sought to replace the emperor with a king of Spain or of France, and ended by finally preparing the scenario for Louis XIV. Giordano Bruno at one time probably placed his hopes in the English crown.

England may seem rather insular, but its archetypes are not altogether different from those of Rome. When the Normans overran the country, the Celts from Brittany who followed them were actually impersonating the archetypal story of the long-delayed revenge of the defeated. The Celtic minstrels provided the Norman monarchy with the myth of King Arthur, who had taken over after Rome had abandoned the island. It became the Tudor knightly myth, and to add strength to it the Augustan myth was duplicated, the founding of London being attributed to a relative of Aeneas, Brut. The Constantinian trick was added: Joseph of Arimathea had brought over for the Arthurian magic bounty at Glastonbury the most precious of Christian relics. The mythical apparel stood the last Tudors and the first Stuart in good stead when they had to rely on their own mythical prestige against the powerful onslaught of the slighted Roman Curia. Spenser, Sidney, and Jonson wove a mantle of melodious verse for the monarchy with all that rich mythical spool. John Dee added the motif of predestined sea-power and of colonial rights inherited from Welsh kings. This was one of the rare new touches in history, though it was actually an appendage to the Celtic fable and to the imperial motif now also coming to the fore in England. It was blended with the preceding settings so well that Blake saw Brut the Trojan in one of his visions:

Hear ye the voice of Brutus: 'The flowing waves
Of time come rolling o'er my breast, he said;
And my heart labours with futurity:
Our sons shall rule the empire of the sea.'

Giordano Bruno had come over to see what could be made of the idea of empire in London, and the Rosicrucians decided to transfer the Holy Roman Empire to an English prince, but the idea of somebody more or less boasting of a homeopathic drop of Trojan blood, back on the throne of the Romans, was ill fated.

England started now on a very insular course, with the Stuarts leaning on the newfangled, shaky myth of a restored Davidic monarchy of neo-Israelites. It was swept away by a formidable new myth of revenge, a 'return of the repressed'. The Saxons had been offstage long enough, so the Parliamentarians rallied to the myth of a return of hardy Saxon democracy and accordingly reshaped the story of England – with the Witenagemot at the beginning, the Magna Charta bringing it back to life, habeas corpus crowning its return and crushing Norman insolence for good. Walter Scott well knew how to exploit the story. But when Cromwell wanted to assert his eminence, he was forced to cull something from the Bible and was no better at it than the uninspired Stuart divines, with his myth of the judges. Ever since, an even balance has been kept, with the Cavaliers harping on Arthurian myths spiced with Augustan–Roman Empire reminiscences, and the Parliamentarians thriving on Saxon democracy. The whole imperial venture was under the star of Rome. (Look up at the inscription under Boadicea's statue when you cross Westminster Bridge.) Kipling drew all the parallels he could, and the question of why Rome fell was always in the minds of Englishmen with an imperial inclination, as though the real historical problem were not the opposite: how Rome could have stood so long.

In *Heart of Darkness* Conrad has Marlow deliver a rambling evocation of all that the estuary of the Thames suggests in the way of archetypes, and Rome comes to the fore:

The Romans first came here nineteen hundred years ago – the other day. . . . Light came out of this river since – you say

> Knights? Yes. . . . We live in the flicker – may it last as long as the old earth keeps rolling! [As for Empire, it] is not a pretty thing when you look into it too much. What redeems it is the idea only . . . not a sentimental pretence, but an idea: and an unselfish belief in the idea – something you can set up, and bow down before, and offer a sacrifice to.

The Augustan dream and the ecclesiastic challenge to its fulfilment were all that Germany was ever treated to, while France, the melting-pot of Celts, Greeks, Latins, Germans, Scandinavians, saw the new myth of nationhood emerge. By the thirteenth century jurists had coined a paradox: the king is emperor in his kingdom, and Paris is another Rome. The ingredients in the fabrication of the mystical body's idiosyncratic identity were remote: the Norman cult of Saint Michael and the Celtic worship of womanhood (France was *douce*). Both were to coalesce in Joan of Arc, who also satisfied people's need to feel arch-Catholic and at the same time at odds with Rome. Shakespeare felt there was an affinity between the 'voices' that guided Joan and the visions of Muhammad. Previously the crusades had helped forge national unity in the same way that warlike expeditions had conflated Islam. The Capets stood by during the process with a medicine pouch ready, their secret coronation ointment in its special vial.

The surge of nationhood brought back to life the most archaic and Platonic of political myths, the triad: the three estates of the realm – clergy, aristocracy, and burghers, over which the king and his crafty lawyers presided. By 1302 the realm was recognised as a corporate or 'mystical' body, a person, whom the king represented. Its enemies were the empire (the Battle of Bouvines disposed of that) and the pontiffs, whose resistance was curbed, so it seems, with the slap of one of the king's lawyers; the papal residence was transferred to Avignon, and the Templars burned at the stake in Place Dauphine. The pull of the older myths, however, proved too strong in the long run, even for the 'sweet' nation of checks and balances combined with strong regal centralisation. Ronsard felt the need to bring in Troy, and Francion, Trojan founder of the Franks; and with Louis XIV the king actually became emperor-like in his imperial palace; his police corps outflanked the intermediary bodies as the Augustan *fiscus* had done with the old Republican institutions of Rome. So much so that when Louis XVI called on the three estates again, a change of archetype had also taken place among the constituents, who were no longer 'the good people of France' – whatever that might mean. The most forceful of them were haunted by the Romulian myth. The work the Jacobins did with archetypes was enormous: they trimmed all the insignia off the old national myth, dismissed the angelic presences; and for all this they substituted, as Disraeli was to say, Romulus. They hacked away not only at statues and paintings but also at the calendar. They altered the musical scales to make sure that the tune would change. (Hobbes had warned against overcultivating Roman history.) Nationhood was scooped empty and filled with a Romulian content. The concoction proved devastating; it spread to all of Europe, where people started noticing their national identity, and in Germany Germanic mythology was added to the brew. This last, however, was an old Roman trick. Tacitus had seen how the element of primeval Germanic hardihood could be grafted on the Romulian mythic stock.

Romulian Paris hardly imagined that it was giving the fatal cue, as always, to its Augustan successor, who promptly followed. Napoleon's staging was so breathtaking that the old dynasty was thrown out of Augustan business for good. He even made sure that this time the pontiff played no tricks, as he had with Charlemagne a thousand years before. The mistake had been to let the pontiff place the crown on the neo-imperial locks, thereby asserting his *Cakravartin* function. Napoleon took the crown in his own hands and placed it on his head himself. Now he was the Roman emperor of the West, with Paris full of sacred objects stolen from Rome. He knew from the ancient script that he had to turn his attention to a rival eastern Rome. In 1453 the second Rome had fallen to the Turks after the pontifical first Rome had crippled it, but its myth had continued – a third Rome was announced in Moscow in 1530. Against this third Rome, the first pontifical Rome had already mounted an assault by her Teuton knights, and later by the Jesuit-inspired conspiracy, which was smashed by Boris Godunov as the first onslaught had been repulsed by (Saint) Alexander Nevsky.

The Romanovs – ironic name – for centuries looked for an opening to get (back, in the mythical sense) to the Bosporus. Napoleon checked the czar's (the Caesar's) moves in that direction at the Tilsit conference, and whispered to his secretary that Constantinople meant world empire. After a long time, Moscow's obsession about the Bosporus came to the fore in exactly the same terms during the twentieth-century talks between Molotov and Ribbentrop.

Napoleon was so keen on arranging things faultlessly that he wrested out of the emperor of Austria the by-then mock title Holy Roman Emperor. He did it in a neatly juridical way that foreclosed all such Hapsburg claims for good.

15 Feeble modern variations

That the democratic tradition in France should be rooted in Romulian myth, while the English tradition was Saxon, has made all the difference in the recent history of the two nations. It also explains why as a whole, despite Carlyle's efforts, the new myth of Germanic fortitude, concomitant with, or opposed to, the Romulian brand, won some hearing in myth-starved nineteenth-century Germany but never gained a footing in England.

The nineteenth century saw the spread of the French Romulian-and-national myth all over Europe. It also reached Italy, which for centuries had been immersed in the myth of the fatherly pontiff caring for his flock (also politically) and in that of empire, with a slender trickle of the Romulian added. The Italian risorgimento hymns are a mixture of the 'return of the repressed' motif (in Garibaldi's hymns tombs are agape and the dead are on their feet again) and of the Romulian mood strangely twisted around to suit the situation (the national anthem runs: 'Italy has clasped on her head Scipio's helmet, because God created her slave to Rome'; the metre is iambic).

Disraeli, an arch-connoisseur of archetypal shifts and balances, foresaw in 1870 exactly what was fated to happen in myth-craving Germany (nowhere else could a grand myth shaper like Wagner appear) and in mythically unstable Italy (which is constantly tempted to give up myth-mongering and fling herself into the arms of some mythically well-assured foreign power). Disraeli warned fifty years too early that the Aryan Germanic myth, with a eugenic twist, would cause an upheaval in German minds and that Italy would try to bring Caesar, the Augustan myth proper, back to life.

If this kind of archetypal calculation had been tried on Russia, it would have clearly emerged that the two myths which dominated the country from its beginning were bound to clash: the dream of the village community, heathen or at least heretically Christian, and the third-Rome Byzantine-Orthodox dream, which at one time even included a fable about the blood of Augustus's brother running in the veins of Rjurik, the Viking founder of czarism. After a brief resurgence of the first myth, the second safely took over.

Out of the whole archetypal history of Europe, the 'return of the repressed' archetype emerges as the most important of all. When the pagan deities, Jupiter and all the Olympians, took over in poetry, painting, and archetypal imagination in general, no sooner were they in state than their magnetism started declining, and those whom they had dethroned loomed large in the imagination of poets, painters, and inspired reformers. Saturn, Prometheus, Astraea emerge in the late Rosicrucian writings and dominate the Romantic mind. As the Augustan myth was being revived by Napoleon – and by English imperialism beyond the Channel – the Romulian myth was gathering unprecedented strength all over Europe, returning finally to its very origins: an appeal to the stragglers, to the disinherited, to all those living on the far fringes of society, that they gather under a harsh leadership. Very often this was a duet of chiefs poised one against the other, and with a plenum Senate appointed to fill the measure of resemblance. Saturn's sickle would undercut Vulcan's, or Thor's, or the woodpecker fraternity's hammer of fecundity. Meanwhile the other myths – of a *Cakravartin* church ready to step into secular concerns, of nationhood, and of Saxon democracy – bide their time. So few are the ruling archetypes when it comes to global political justification. The hieratic Egyptian system and the myth of Alexander end by falling into the Augustan pattern; the Spartan model is absorbed into the Romulian; the Athenian into the Saxon. When Europeans are confronted with loose, easy political systems of shamanistic peoples, sometimes entirely based on seership, they compulsively construe them as variants of the savage Romulian model.

It is extraordinary how the magic circle woven round political imagination coerces minds and can appear unchangeable. Nothing seems to be conceivable beyond the few appeals that can be classed (if one prefers to use the classical sevenfold planetary scale) as the Romulian junction of Saturn and Mars, the Augustan combination of Apollo and Jupiter with Venus, the checks and balances of Mercury, the moon of nationhood. One additional cluster sticks out of the frame: the Saturnian vision of an impending social or cosmic earthquake and of the ensuing redemptive renewal. Certain religious systems incorporate its appeal, and apply to the 'redeemed' world the adjectives and the imagery that are associated with metaphysical experience. This is true especially of Zoroastrianism, hence of Shiah Islam, and of Judaism. It seems to have been part and parcel of early Christianity – the Book of Revelation especially was interpreted as an announcement of destruction-cum-renovation for the near future – and in the Middle Ages even the Trinity was more or less heretically keyed to the tune, with the two dispensations of the Father and of the Son condemned to be superseded by the kingdom of the Holy Ghost. With certain Anabaptists the archetype made a bid for power, but owing to its very nature its political usefulness could not outlast the rule of a provisional committee. Even when shorn of its religious connotation as utopian socialism, the archetype cannot warrant anything more than very short-lived governments, readily replaced by Romulian or Augustan tinctures.

This latter, ephemeral, intermittent political archetype of Europe – revolt-that-pretends-to-be-Apocalypse – was caught in the net of a painter's brush strokes and now hangs in the Kunstmuseum of Dusseldorf. It was first exhibited in 1851 in Berlin, while the echo of the German 1848 revolt was lingering in the atmosphere. The artist, Johan Peter Hasenclever, was at the peak of his activity. He died two years later. He had painted 'meaningful', often humorous scenes, in the detailed, realistic style of the Dusseldorf school, but here he accomplishes the most lofty task of immobilising that Proteus: a living, relatively infinite archetype. The scene takes place in the meeting-room of a German municipality around 1848. At the centre a large window opens onto the town square, thronged with demonstrators. On the left a deputation stands facing the town councillors, seated at their table on the right. The chief delegate from the lower estates waves a petition; he seems stunned at his own daring – a huge fellow, shaky on his legs. One of his companions bares his teeth in a saucy, sinister grin, pointing with his thumb at the crowd in the square. Another is striking an inspired pose – a handsome young man in whose ear a sallow, ill-shaven ideologue is whispering something.

The town council forms a kind of circle at whose centre the secretary is seated; a lanky, pale-faced man frozen by fear, he has just stopped penning the minutes. An enormous burgher, sitting with legs spread out under his bulging belly, stares vacantly, passing a handkerchief over his brow. An elderly man is signifying with his hands something like 'Gentlemen, please look at the balance sheet; there's no room for further expenditure.' One councillor is leaning against the wall and seems captivated by the rebels. Another, bent over the table, eyes aglare at them, must have just clinched in his mind the plan for a counter-thrust. Only after taking in each single character does one start noticing the background. The walls are hung with archducal or princely portraits, some of them aslant; and in a dark corner stands a suit of medieval plate-armour, with the councillors' top hats thrust over the helmet and the shoulder pieces, an umbrella dangling from the brassard. A whole lesson *a parte* on feudal survivals versus the early manufacturing classes – in a few neat, penumbral dabs.

The scene has been played over and over again, from Masaniello's seventeenth-century Neapolitan revolt to student riots in our century, to all possible political tunes, with all kinds of pretexts. But when the archetype does pounce on a community and holds it in its clutches, then there is no escape, whatever the motivations and backgrounds. Here one is, having no choice, obliged to step into one of the roles in the picture, having to go through the gestures that Hasenclever depicted once and for all. Such is the force of an archetype at work; a Rorschach test is being served us.

16 Political archetypes are degenerations

And yet all these political archetypes that so firmly hold the West in their airy grip are but a degenerate version of metaphysical stories. The deepest secret of history is this – that sometimes the enlightened, on returning to an earthly level, feel the urge to somehow convey their experience. Call the urge Bodhisattvic mercy or saintly charity or the sheer flow of metaphysical poetry; the result is a cosmogony – after all the world was started when light was made in the soul – a story of gods creating or sacrificing or loving or fighting. The story's upshot is by definition unintelligible to the layman, and in his fatal misinterpretation it ends up by becoming the mysterious foundation myth of a political system: the explanation, the justification of authority. No proviso on the part of the enlightened myth-maker will avoid the lapse. Even the Kingdom-within-you of Christianity, born of the specific rejection of political Messiahdom, turned into the justification of the Holy Roman Empire; just as the message of deliverance of the Lord Buddha had become the sustaining myth of Eastern Kingdoms. Of course even these betrayals could be defended by asking: 'Who is going to provide a shelter for the teaching?' A *defensor fidei* feels that the myth he defends should serve as his mythical defence.

Politics is incapable of finding its justification in itself. It has to impinge on metaphysics. The dregs of metaphysical experience become the apology of Empire.

At two removes symbolical recitals dealing with ineffable illumination become expendable political archetypes; multitudes are spellbound, united by the last refraction of what originally was the light of supreme knowledge.

Tell the story of the One that turns into the Many and it shall become that of the One Tribe, of the Divine King, of the Perfect Unifying System in the throes of history. Mystical truths become political mystifications, metaphysical similes practical rallying cries. One reason why Vedânta appeals so strongly is that its formulas have for so long avoided conscription into political service.

Even the Romulian myth, the strongest in Western political imagination, derives its appeal from an originally cosmic myth, which justifies not a State but the All. The Twins are dual Unity, yin–yang emerging on the waters of the Beginning, out of the fluid potentiality of existence. The story runs that Vishnu as a child was washed by the waters of the deluge into the branches of a banyan tree, the Bengal fig tree, which is the centre of Hindu villages and the emblem of Unity in multiplicity. In Sanskrit *ashvin* are the twins and *ashvatta* is the fig tree of Life. The twins in the Tree of Life are the two birds of the Upanishad, of which one eats the fruits of the tree of life, and represents all-devouring Fire, while the other looks on meekly, like the Sun. The Tree of Life is Light as such, invisible light-giving Light. Remus eats, transgresses and is sacrificed by the Law-giver Sun-king Romulus. The same setting of the Tree appears in a not so very different dramatic cycle, in which the onlooker-Sun is the Father, and the eater is his son Prometheus or Lucifer, who brings the Father's essence down among us, and is born of the friction of wood or of a stone, and should be anointed with fuel – forming the Triad of Sun, Fire and Wind which are One. The story takes on the strangest shapes, borrows the most recondite elements. It turns up in the Middle Ages in the vision of the Tree of Life as a Burning Bush with the Twins – God and the Serpent – amid the flames. It changes like a dream sequence. On the highest level it signifies metaphysical experience – Oneness – but from below it signifies the only form of oneness inferior minds can conceive, social unifying power.

Political myths are fallen, degraded empyrean visions. As those who cannot transcend their person conceive of Oneness as God-*the*-Person, according to His various attributes or archetypes, those who cannot even go beyond their historical political *persona* end by reducing the divine archetypes to the unifying political identities of an era. Even the archetype of Revolution-as-apocalypse was in origin as it appeared – in its purity – to metaphysically inspired Wordsworth, when in the apocalyptic, awesome clash of the winds at the Simplon Pass he descried

> The types and symbols of Eternity
> Of first, and last, and midst, and without end.

IV *Archetypal Poetry*

17 Archetypes and poetry. Silence is the matrix

> The ancient Poets animated all sensible objects with Gods or Geniuses, calling them by names and adorning them with the properties of woods, rivers, mountains, lakes, cities, nations and whatever their enlarged & numerous senses could perceive.
>
> And particularly they studied the genius of each city & country, placing it under its mental deity;
>
> Till a system was formed, which some took advantage of, & enslav'd the vulgar by attempting to realize or abstract the mental deities from their objects; thus began Priesthood;
>
> Choosing forms of worship from poetic tales.

These lines of Blake's *Marriage of Heaven and Hell* are of such consequence that a history of the world could hinge on them. In their light poetry appears to have only one possible subject – archetypes.

Poetry may be defined as the art of describing archetypes by seeing, to use a Blakean phrase, not with the eyes but through them. To achieve this, the poet must rise from deeper down – or descend from higher up – than the archetypal level; he must have sounded the rock-bottom of absolute silence, because only from there can archetypes be viewed properly.

What essence is to substance, what the weft is to the web, silence is to poetry.

A poem is a statement about something unutterable; it is silence underscored with words, words offered up in sacrifice to silence.

The ineffable is the only fit subject of great poetry and poetry often consists of a string of questions that are invocations to silence: Who will tell? How shall I speak? To what shall I compare?

Silence is not only what precedes and follows poetry, the moment of expectation at the beginning and the lingering silent rapture at the end. It is what poetry is basically about, what interpenetrates and activates poetry.

Expressive, significant silence intimates the notion of undivided oneness that cannot be properly denoted by language, which is fundamentally dyadic, based on the binary relation of a predicate and a subject. Language cannot connote oneness, absolute unity, otherwise than by negating itself, through silence. When it does so – paradoxically – in words, endeavouring to transcend itself without ceasing to be itself, it becomes poetry.

On the other hand language finds difficulty in expressing negation directly. Poetry, which negates ordinary language, is actually overstressed language pointing to what is beyond and prior to itself.

The main, typical subject of archaic poetry was cosmogony, the description of how being stems from non-being, multiplicity from undivided oneness, the Word from utter silence. The story of how the universe came into being was felt to be the proper subject whenever the occasion called for a return to the origin of all, for an act of solemn, healing centring.

The Trojan singers that follow Aeneas entertain the wandering party with the story of the world, as the *scops* do among king Hrothgar's retinue in *Beowulf*. It is fit that English literature should begin with Caedmon's new song of creation.

The greatest of questions, the prime and ultimate enigma, is the emergence of being out of nothingness. Only poetry can tackle it.

On the lowest level of interpretation a cosmogony is the factual account of what took place at the beginning of beginnings. But, since a beginning can take place only *in* time, there can be no beginning *of* time. As history, cosmogonies are absurd.

On a higher level cosmogonies depict the inner experience of the implications of the idea of being, and describe in terms of a myth, of a story, the conceptual substructure of reality. Cosmogonies in this sense can only be composed in poetry, because they transcend the world they seek to explain. Poetry is in itself the best example of silence flowering into words, the choicest means of expression for the metaphysical notion of non-being sprouting into being. The zero point of cosmogony is also the core of poetry; poetry is what cosmogony is about: it is silence speaking, the void giving birth to being.

18 Cosmogony as aesthetics

The totality of being is unutterable: it is absolute silence, which is the starting-point of all cosmogonies.

The Christian genesis is no exception, though the Gospel of St John places at the beginning the Word, *logos*. In the Eastern Church the icon of St John of Silence is worshipped, in which the apostle holds his Gospel open at the first page – 'In the beginning there was the Word' – while pressing his curled fingers to his lips, signifying silence. He is cross-eyed, signifying the inward gaze. A winged figure is whispering something in his ear. It is Divine Wisdom, Sophia.

Commentators claim that the icon should be referred to the last words of the Gospel, which are a self-transcendence of the Gospel; they state that nobody could write down the words of the resurrected Word incarnate: 'If they should be written down even the world itself could not contain the books that should be written.'

Given the common nexus with silence, cosmogonies are the key to poetry; they are actually treatises on poetry.

In Vedic cosmogony, which is paradigmatic, this is explicit. It places at the beginning, at the essence of reality, silence, death.

Silence starts vibrating.

The vibration becomes a rhythm, hence a network of interlacing rhythmic patterns. Then these become luminous and visible forms, and take on shapes whose inner core is what preceded them: their pulse, the cosmic rhythm reverberating in them.

This precedence of sound and rhythm over visible appearances was a matter of daily observation. Was it not the imitation of their voice and gait that attracted, allured animals? Was not the perception of rhythms in nature the key to changes in the environing world? Were not lullabies, drummings, tomtoms, death chants the most intimate modes of communication?

The story of beginnings or essences could also be told with another set of similes, according to which the universe is a Cosmic Man. Probably the etymon of 'world' bears witness to this peculiar cosmological metaphor: *wer*, 'man'; *ald*, 'old', 'big'.

At the beginning Cosmic Man sacrificed himself so that the world should be. Or demons slaughtered him. We now dwell amid his strewn, dead limbs. But when we collect ourselves inwardly, fleeing the sight of a dead world, we recollect the beginning; the living Cosmic Man is resurrected in us.

The primal rhythmic patterns are his spine; his limbs, branching out, form the various hymns. When his acoustic, poetic body is completed, he becomes visible: poetry is, as the etymon states, the making of reality.

The experience of the poet is that of Cosmic Man. It starts with a sheer silence, a dedicated listening, which allows the vibrations, the rhythms of reality, the pulse of beings to emerge and roll through the poet's heart and mind; he then feels words flowing, clothing the rhythms.

Vedânta teaches us to count the phases of cosmogony.

There's the zero phase of silence, from which explodes the all-comprehensive, total, unitary and therefore inaudible word – *sphota*, from the root *sphu* 'explode', 'spout'. Then, a thundering, rumbling whirl starts rotating, impelled by the compressed energy of *sphota*, the spouting energy of the unsounded word. This vortex, at phase three, develops articulate rhythms. One, two, three: one – the silent *sphota*, or spout of manifestation; two – the first rumbling of its self-reflection; which becomes three – articulate rhythmic life. One – silent being. Two – the reflection of being, knowledge. Three – the bliss of rhythm unfolding. And the three are one. Thus in man *sphota* (the inaudible word) is a spouting, a surging at the root of the spine, an obscure pulsion. It rises in the belly, it is distinctly perceived; it reaches the heart, where it becomes a rhythm, a metre.

Phase four: the sleeping cosmos is stirred by the first eruption of sound; from the heart the utterance has reached the throat, becoming audible.

Phase five: in the twilit, dreaming, poetic cosmos, the word resonates; words are said to issue forth from the lips, mounted on the divine bird Garuda; poetic words are winged like birds or darts. At this point the world is not yet severed, distinct from the poet, from the singer who rapturously praises, caresses its emerging twilight shapes.

Six: now the world stands out revealed, in full view, an endless multiplicity of separate entities, and poetry ceases. The visible, fallen world of contrasts such as we know it, takes over. But still we can intermittently detach ourselves from it; we call on the poet, and his winged words lead us back towards the silence from which the all arose.

Poetry, according to Hindu metaphysics, is language that no longer consists of mere phonemes and socially accepted meanings, but emphasises their resonance. The Sanskrit word is *dhvani*. Commentators are careful to stress that it is neither the sound nor the meaning of the word, but rather its suffusion, the vibrating psychic halo around it, which is the effect of convergence and context. 5,355 ways of making mere words resonate were listed by Vedantic metaphysicians.

Dhvani is not mere emotion. It conveys an objective cognition of what we might call an archetype – a generative, shaping essence which is objective and subjective at the same time. It is not emotion, though it is coloured by emotion, and it is not a set of facts as such, but what animates them. The sense of poetical resonance or suggestivity is called 'taste', 'flavour' or 'juice' (*rasa*).

Poetry then is the resonance of language that conveys the flavours of reality. It is distinct from ordinary, non-suggestive, non-resonant language and its flavoured otherwordly (*lokottara*) reality differs from the common tasteless round of existence.

Poetic resonance is what a word is in the heart, before it is voiced in the throat: an unworded throb brimming with import and significance, but as yet unreferred to a formal, stiff, pigeon-hole meaning, and to a specific phoneme. Specifications are always fraught with arbitrariness and never do full justice to what the heart enshrined: the seed, the energy gushing fresh out of the sheer, powerful latency of silence, out of the core of our, of cosmic being.

The waking scene of visible forms is a dead world, which is no sooner focused than it has already slipped away, and words only grasp it insofar as it belongs to the past. It is poetry that can capture the quiver, the glint of instant revelation, the unspoilt nowness, the keen flavour of existence at its awakening out of the all-enfolding cosmic silent sleep.

Vedantic theories of poetry speak of eight flavours or archetypes; they must not be rigidly defined in words, but only tasted in the resonance of words.

First comes the archetype of comicality; to get its flavour, one is invited to think of the colour white, to consider that demons instil it; it fosters silliness and cleverness, outrageousness, peals of laughter, chattiness, nonsense, sleep. Next come emerald green, pleasure-bestowing eros; pigeon-grey pathos; crimson wrath; tawny bravery; black horror; disgusting indigo; and finally the yellow sense of the marvellous whose cause is the Creator himself. Pavel Florensky's theory of colour proves useful at this point; colour is the best symbol for resonance, since it results from white-golden light encountering earthly dust in mid-air, and resonating as indigo when it clashes against it, as redness when it penetrates it, as green when the two are balanced.

At the centre from which the circle of all archetypes fans out is the flavour of quietude, the silent bliss and knowledge that accompany the taste of poetic resonance even when the subject is painful or disgusting.

19 Poetry and symmetry

Poetry, which implies an unusually warm, intimate involvement with objects, at the same time makes for detachment, because it focuses on the archetypes beyond them. A poetic response to life is glowing and vibrating, but it is directed to what lies beyond the direct immediacy of objects, to the generative, tone-setting pattern both of the object and of the reactions to it.

The poet's logic is that of the unconscious, which does not separate things from their engendering gender. The lover, whose mind follows the same logic, perceives the beloved as merging into the archetype of loveliness, not as the mere cluster of her specific attributes. Likewise, a man overwhelmed by fear is not moved by the specifically frightening elements of a situation, but by fear itself as the class of all fearful things.

Henry James described this sheer flavour of the nightmarish archetype in *The Beast in the Jungle*, as he studied the pure archetype of pleasure in *The Nice Good Place*, and of ghastliness in *The Turn of the Screw*.

This blending of objects into their archetype is, according to Melanie Klein, the chief trait of the world of the child, which feels its bowel movements as the very power to crash and blast, its wish to bite as the power of dismembering living bodies.

Every night we return to this condition in dreams. But, as Keats warned, the poet is the opposite of the hazy dreamer. He places himself at the level of reality from which and out of which dreams arise; he assumes the role of the mysterious agency that shapes our dreams, whose procedures he adopts, from synechdoche to metonymy, from contraction to displacement.

The poet is not a dreamer, but a maker of dreams. He weaves nightmares and swoons, and he communicates not only their taste but also the flavour of his craftsmanly quiet, appreciative competence and control.

Contact with the logic of dreams – or of love or of terror or of schizophrenia – makes us anxious and fretful; we then react by overasserting, stressing the other's otherness. The poet instead quietly accepts the otherness; he never forgets that the foundations of waking life lie in the cosmogonic phase that preceded it. He refuses to privilege the binary logic, the either-ors of our waking state.

The logic of the dreamer and of the schizophrenic – of the subconscious – is based, according to Ignacio Mate Blanco, on two rules:

a) A thing is tantamount to its class, and each class is tantamount to a wider class. Classes can be persons. This is a formulation of what can also be called the focusing of archetypes.

b) A relation is coincidental with its contrary, with which it forms a symmetrical couple. So every relation is reflected in its opposite as in a looking-glass and symmetrical logic replaces binary logic.

On this rule of the logic of dreaming states, retaliation, revenge and commutative justice are based. Their appeal is a call from dreamland. Also the symmetry of verses and refrains answers to the principle.

The first rule is adopted by the poet when he deals with parts as though they were the whole set to which they belong, and this is why we feel a funny, slight poetic thrill when instead of 'fifty ships' we say 'fifty sail', or instead of 'king' or 'monarchy' or 'royal house', we opt for 'the crown'. This also explains why twins are so often considered disturbing, to the point that normal binary logic is reinstated symbolically by sacrificing one of them. The foreskin, which evokes symmetrical femininity, is considered equally alarming. On the other hand, the logic of the unconscious works both ways, and what is alarming becomes symmetrical to what is reassuring, so the caul takes the place of the twin as the sign of the guardian spirit or double, or a doll is made of the deceased twin and treated with worshipful solicitude.

Poe's Wilson and all the *Doppelgänger* evoke the alarming and alluring shudder of symmetry. A symmetrical universe cannot be ordered into a chain of individual events. Poets do not panic at the perspective; they bundle together symmetrical realities with loose chains of binary logic and with the non-verbal assertion of unity – which is the unifying formal pattern of the poem, its rhythmical structure and its fundamental tonal blend. This poetic unity is cogent not morally or from the point of view of contrastive logic, but from that of a harmonious balance of contrastive and of symmetrical logic, thanks to which a practically infinite multiplicity of symmetries, like mirrored mirrorings, are unified to reveal a common archetype and its flavour.

Total symmetry would coincide with sleep or coma; poetry skims them, and we feel thrilled.

Totalitarian binary logic would on the other hand coincide with an absolute totality and unity, so its end result also would be oneness, silence, and absolute symmetry. Poets have often chosen this paradox as their theme.

Blake's realm of Urizen, Ahab's dream of a totalitarian cartography of the oceans, Valéry's ideal of absolute control whose result is ecstasy – all lead us into a universe of total symmetrical logic.

20 Poetry and synchronicity

Jung taught that the approach of an archetype creates synchronicities, that the psychic vortex it creates is like an axle, an axis of symmetry between outward reality and inward experience.

Poetry can be defined as the language of synchronicity and of coincidence as against the causality of everyday reality; it is assumed in poetry that landscapes are coincidental with man's feelings, metric patterns with subject-matter.

In synchronicity what happens happens because it happens now. The nowness is the explanation; past and future are symmetrical and the present is their axis of symmetry. Also in poetry the past and the future revolve on the present instant as its bilateral projections. In *A Defence of Poetry* Shelley claimed that 'a poet participates in the eternal, the infinite, the one . . . As far as he relates to his conceptions, time and place and number are not. The grammatical forms which express the modes of time and the difference of persons, and the distinction of place, are convertible in respect to the highest poetry, without injuring it as poetry.'

Synchronicity is the experience in which the idea of divination is rooted; a fall of dice and the ideas that concurrently emerge in the thrower's psyche are supposed to belong to the same plexus, to show forth the same archetype.

Poetry was born as the oracular response of the evoked archetype. It is intimately linked with divination and enigmas, as Plato recalls in *Alcibiades*. Contemplation turns a scene into an enigma, into an archetype, which is always half-submerged. Poetry answers the query of the enigma in the form of a myth. When the object of contemplation is the whole world, the answer is a cosmogony.

In places where poetry is still a festal occasion and a communal feast, as in the Italian region of Tuscia, the relation is apparent. Poetic contests start with a challenge. One poet will sing the praises of water and dare another to extol earth – any couple of opposites will do – until one of them is silenced, having outrun his store of similes, of rhymes, of enthusiasm. The winner's last dashing couplet carries the day, wins the wager, gives the response, solves the riddle, turns the symmetrical into a binary couple, decides what side of the opposition is to be sacrificed.

Poets in Tuscia are mostly charcoal-burners, who have time to meditate in silence in the forest. When they abandon the silent retreat and display their art, they put themselves in the right spirit by drinking the right amount of wine, neither too much nor too little, neither total symmetry nor total contrastiveness. When a whiff of inspiration is nearing, coincidences crop up. A charcoal-burner confided to me: 'I was thinking of a little boy who had just died, when I saw a butterfly taking to its wings from off the bark of a nearby tree; to the rhythm of its flight a poem gushed forth, linking the boy's and the butterfly's departure.'

21 Poetry and suggestivity

The Sanskrit *dhvani*, 'resonance', can also be translated as 'suggestivity'. The term can now be used in more than just a suggestive way, since G. Lozanov has distilled its essence, neatly separating it from hypnosis, which implies a loss of consciousness; from persuasion, which is the effect of words and meanings, rather than overtones; and finally from strictly logical cogency.

Suggestion is what happens when a message is received by a mind fully aware, but fluctuating from one flux of messages to another. In this condition the suggestion is taken in by the mind and it can penetrate to the deepest strata of memory. As when a shuttle shoots the weft thread through the opening of a web, when the mind shifts from one to the other layer of perception, a suggestion penetrates to the very core of memorisation. The art of suggestion will therefore present the mind with a series of parallel different fluxes of communication, so that it opens intermittently to the 'weft threads'. As a result the mind will be impressed with the suggested message the way a fabric is marked by its weft. The art of suggestology is currently applied to teaching languages and to psychotherapy. The feel of a language, along with its vocabulary, or a new organising principle for the disturbed mind, can be insinuated by the orchestration of a series of communications. Music, well modulated speech, the interplay of group relationships, and the playing of roles are combined and enmeshed so that a strongly motivated mind will intently and relaxedly follow the various messages, easily opening up, as a web separates its threads, to the pedagogical or therapeutic intimation. Poetry arranges the same kind of mesh, plaiting together its rhythms, its phonetic patterns, the metrical expectations, the meanings and the submeanings. The factual communication, the apparent, obvious message of the poem, through its metrical effects, is refracted, and the archetypal gist is suggested slipped through.

Wordsworth analysed this suggestological method of refraction in his preface to *Lyrical Ballads*, pointing out that metre divests language of its full reality, casting 'a sort of half-conciousness of insubstantial existence over the whole composition'.

This explains why poetry, more than prose, enables us to endure painful, pathetic and even horrifying descriptions. The metric intertexture diverts the mind from the communications at hand, tempering pathos with distance, overshadowing participation with appreciation.

The refracted binary logic of the subject matter, of the obvious plot, is placed on the same level with all other elements; as T. S. Eliot said, it can be put in just to satisfy the reader's habit, keeping his mind diverted and calm while the poem does its work on him. We are now in a position to define what Eliot called 'the poem' as the flavour of the archetype lying behind the plot and subject matter.

Henry James devoted his whole life to stressing the point; his *The Art of Fiction* is particularly useful. The various elements – description proper, method, dialogue, incident – are subordinated to the central suggestion. People are used to talking of such things as if they had 'a kind of internecine distinctness', whereas they melt into each other at every breath, being associated parts of one general 'effort of expression'. Each function is spliced with every other, producing the one and continuous flavour in whose close texture one cannot trace a definite 'geography of items', a strict binary logic.

In terms of cosmogony poetry can be said to throw into relief the vibrations of the word on the level of the heart, where the purely rhythmic, generating patterns form; and on a yet deeper level it gives the feel of the stirring primal archetypal force, the hum in the very veins at the core of being, where being emerges from silence.

The greater the poetry, the more it opens like a maelstrom onto the very foundations of silent nothingness which is also the inconceivable totality of being.

This can only be achieved in a state of suggestibility created by means of an intoxicatingly multilevelled structure, in which the imagination is called on to implement, as Cullen Bryant wrote, the glimpses, gleams, traces and dashes of the poem, while attention is being incessantly shifted from one level of communication to the next, until the rhythm, and below that, the essential shaping form or archetype occupies the centre of the picture. This is achieved by refractions and diversions that generate a suggestive aura, which carries the taste of the central archetype.

22 Poetry as an experience of archetypes

That poetry introduces us to archetypes is made clear by all the great English Romantic poets.

Coleridge in his discussion of the *Lyrical Ballads* talks about poetry exciting 'a feeling analogous to the supernatural by awakening the mind's attention from the lethargy of custom', by 'lifting the film of familiarity'.

Shelley in *A Defence of Poetry* speaks of poets 'drawing into a certain propinquity with the beautiful and the true, that partial apprehension of the agencies of the invisible world which is called religion. Hence all original religions are allegorical or susceptible of allegory, and, like Janus, have a double face, false and true.'

Keats in *Endymion* also taught how the poetic apprehension of archetypes may be achieved in the only way such an art can be imparted; he prescribed that one smoothe one's lips with a roseleaf, listen to melodious winds, sense prophecy in mute things – put oneself in a suggestible condition.

> Feel we these things? that moment have we stepped
> Into a sort of oneness, and our state
> Is like a floating spirit's.

When one is in such a condition, akin to that which old hypnotists induced with intermittent lights, or with crystal balls, the archetypes will be revealed – friendship's steady splendour, or the orbed drop of light, love, in whose radiance we blend and are renewed, beyond all chaff of custom, of what Coleridge called the lethargy of custom.

The poet is 'possessed' by the archetype. The approach of the archetype creates the thrill of poetry.

When the participants in cults of spirit-possession feel the approach of the god, of the personified archetype, such as in voodoo the love goddess Erzulie, or the death-god Baron Samedi, they are slightly intoxicated, a sort of tingling sensation runs through their body. As the sensation grows they start jerking, their hair stands on end, and consciousness founders. Poetry rarely reaches these extremes. It gives the taste of the god or archetype, without blotting out the listener's awareness.

Poetry is born from the shaman's experience of controlled possession; he is perfectly alert while his whole being feels the god or archetype, while his imagination hallucinates to convey the figures that help gravitate towards the archetype.

Poetry is, in Keats's words, a 'rich entanglement' – so rich that it brings into play even the unnameable, silent stirrings of the unconscious. It is always more than the poet controls.

23 Poetry and symbols

A poem is about archetypes, which are relative infinities, just as the colours the spectrum refracts out of sheer white light are, each one of them, relatively infinite groupings of tints.

Things and beings mentioned in the plot of a poem are symbols of the ineffable, relatively infinite archetype. Poets have tried at times to explain this capital and elusive aspect of their craft.

Conrad made a brave endeavour to show the archetypal presences behind the objects of a poetic narrative in *Heart of Darkness*, in his description of the voice of the mysterious mistress of Kurtz the adventurer: 'The sound of her low voice seemed to have the accompaniment of all other sounds, full of mystery, desolation, and sorrow, I had ever heard – the ripple of the river, the sighing of the trees swayed by the wind, the murmur of the crowds, the faint ring of incomprehensible words cried from afar, the whisper of a voice speaking from beyond the threshold of an eternal darkness.'

The mere voice, thanks to context and convergence, becomes the symbol of the archetype looming above the entire book, the embodiment of the primal cosmogonic nightwood roar. It answers Leibniz's definition of a monad: a point of view on the all, infinity in a point, the infinite as a point. A sign, the woman's particular timbre of voice, is turned into a fully fledged, partially unutterable symbol by means of a suggestive orchestration that lifts it beyond its mere factual existence, shuttles it into the depths of the memorising, imaginative faculty. All equally momentous imaginable analogues will gravitate round it.

It now answers Goethe's definition of a symbol, as distinct from a sign, which is the mere communication of a given content; and as distinct from allegory, which is a cool, conscious, open, single-tracked operation. The famous definition can be found in *Maximen und Reflexionen*: a symbol is not the dreamy, vague shadow of a thing, but 'a living instantaneous revelation of the inscrutable', which shows forth the archetype or idea 'in such a way that the idea remains always infinitely active and unapproachable in its image'.

Any poem is an illustration of the various points touched on, but Dylan Thomas's masterpiece is as explicit as a treatise.

> The force that through the green fuse drives the flower
> Drives my green age; that blasts the roots of trees,
> Is my destroyer.
> And I am dumb to tell the crooked rose
> My youth is bent by the same wintry fever.

The archetype of growth appears in symmetric logic, both life-bestowing and death-dealing, as intoxicating and heart-rending as all the symbols that have represented it through the ages, from the green face of Osiris onwards.

The archetypal truth is reiterated by the images, from that of the sap blasting its way up the roots to the stalk sorrowfully bent under the burden of the full-blown rose; so rich is their blend that it projects beyond them, into the sheer mystery of growth and of origins. Plotinus said (II, 9, 16): 'When one sees in an object the outward portrayal of an archetype, the heart is shaken and the memory of the Original recaptured.'

All contrastive logic ceases, even the dichotomies of good and evil, which in normal conditions represent the primal question. Thomas offers us fruits from the tree of life. Those from the tree of the knowledge of good and evil open the eyes but close the innocent heart that knows nothing of good and evil, as Baudelaire explained in that sweet booming address: 'O Beauty, do you come from out of the deep sky, or do you issue forth from the abyss? Your gaze, hellish and divine, pours out in confusion both boon and crime, and we shall therefore compare you with wine.'

In Thomas's poem the refrain is an obsessive reiteration of the heart's dumbness, which is one with the ineffability, the silence at the core of poetry. In the first stanza the poet is dumb to tell the rose that they are one.

> And I am dumb to mouth unto my veins
> How at the mountain spring the same mouth sucks.

The fused green drive becomes the equally ineffable suction of the red aspiring heart. Opposites blend:

> And I am dumb to tell the hanging man
> How of my clay is made the hangman's lime.

And finally, the poet is dumb to tell the lover's tomb that the same round worm is eating away at his sheet. The curl of the worm, the bend of the rose-stalk evoke the age-old emblem, the closed ring of death and marriage.

In the poem not only are the conscious plot and the unconscious reverberations on the same footing, but the unconscious psyche is at the same time dumb nature, in an unutterable blending of subject and object, about which the poet is 'dumb to tell' because, with the interfusion of subject and object, the silence, the inarticulateness of objects, seeps through into him. The mute stones and clouds which his gaze absorbs transmute him to their likeness. He pays for his penetration into nature by becoming, like nature herself, unfathomably reticent, by realising that he is impelled by unformulable drives. Baudelaire spoke about the poet's idiotic look, the famous *air bête*.

The poet is mineral-like, vegetable-like, because in him and for him the mystery of nature and the secrets of the unconscious are one and the same. A mute stone is a signifier of his unconscious, stone-like psyche, of what Freud called It, and the result is a sense of unutterable hovering archetypes. In the iconography of Chinese literature there is the motif of the poet Mi Fu bowing to a hill as to a brother.

'What have those lonely mountains worth revealing?' asks Emily Brontë, and answers: 'More glory and more grief than I can tell.'

There is the famous passage in Wordsworth's *Prelude*:

> To every natural form, rock, fruits, or flowers,
> Even the loose stones that cover the highway,
> I gave a moral life; I saw them feel,
> Or linked them to some feeling; the great mass
> Lay bedded in a quickening soul, and all
> That I beheld respired with inward meaning.

This poetic idiocy or dumbness rejoins the notion of the symbol as distinct from a mere sign. C. G. Jung explained that in a symbol a mystery of the physical world and an unfathomable psychic latency coalesce. He gave the telling example of the loaf of bread, which, with a proper orchestration, thanks to a liturgy, becomes the symbol of the physical mystery: the growth of wheat, its transformation into a loaf transformed by leaven, flavoured by its empty parts; and at the same time symbolises a psychic mystery: its physical substance, digested, distilled into subtle, psychic matter, is made one with the very mind that meditates on its symbolicity. The loaf of Aztec and Christian liturgical poems can also serve as the arch-symbol of the fundamental fact of poetry: the blending of the subject and the object, the animation of nature and the quietening of a psyche safely anchored to nature.

In *Lines Composed a Few Miles above Tintern Abbey* Wordsworth describes the groundwork of poetry as

> A motion and a spirit that impels
> All thinking things, all objects of all thoughts,
> And rolls through all things.

Only resonance can convey the motion and spirit.

24 Poetry, inscape and myth

A poet becomes part and parcel of outward nature to such an extent that he learns to observe objectively, as a natural phenomenon, what goes on within his psyche, behind the trains of images and feelings and thoughts that flit over the screen of his mind. As in a shadow-show he descries the puppeteer-archetype, and this makes for a detachment which is not to be confused with coldness or apathy.

A poet is at white heat, as Emily Dickinson was fond of repeating; his lucidity is that of intolerable intensity.

When he focuses his inner world he clearly sees the various persons or component parts, and realises the moving agencies that hold sway over them; his spiritual anatomy is clearly outlined; the simile of the theatre or of the puppet-show comes naturally to him.

This clear inward vision may explain the astounding persistence of certain stock metaphors through the ages.

Ananda Coomaraswamy examined these recurring metaphors. Among them is the simile of the string that draws man's psyche heavenward, from the golden cord with which Zeus draws all things to himself in the *Iliad* (VIII, 18) to the golden cord to which Plato says we puppets should hold fast (*Laws* 644). Shams-i-Tabrîzî, Hafîz, Dante (*Paradise* I, 116) are other examples. Chuang-tzu's thread of life is the same thread of the spirit fastened to the Sun in the *Shatapatha Brâhmana*, as also the thread of the cosmic necklace in the *Bhagavad Gîta*. In *Vedânta* speech is the cord, names are the knots that tie things to it. All gloriously re-emerges in Blake:

I give you the end of a golden string,
Only wind it into a ball;
It will lead you at heaven's gate
Built in Jerusalem's wall.

To Coomaraswamy's bounty, no end of sheaves can be added. The Greeks spoke of the binding thread of destiny, and tragic necessity they called the Strangling Thread (*Anankê*). The world's axis is the spindle of Necessity; second sight enables us to see its threads, the yarns it spins.

The Hindu poet of the *Atharva Veda* (VI, 121) prays that the knots of evil-dreaming and adversity be untied, as the Greek poet invokes Dionysus the loosener.

Since a poet is bound to fix his gaze beyond the reach of the puppets, and to follow the strings that move their limbs up to the archetype that controls them, and since the archetype is realised and understood at the deepest pyschic levels only if it is personified, it follows that a poet needs a mythology, a pantheon, as much as his ancestor the shaman did.

A shared, communally accepted pantheon is of immense aid to a poet. The current, arid treatises of mythology come alive, bigger than life, in the imagination of poets – Keats and Shelley in their time as much as Eliot and Pound in theirs. Such is the need poets feel for what Robinson Jeffers, in *Roan Stallion*, called 'the phantom rulers of humanity', which, without shape, shape things – the shadows of things that shadow things forth, 'to whom temples, to whom churches, to whom labors and wars, visions and dreams are dedicated'.

The discussions of the use of mythology in the eighteenth century missed the point; it is a shallow time when Johnson complains about the mythography of Milton's *Lycidas* and Addison condescendingly admits of the use of myth in mock-heroic poems.

It is a grand and rare feat of the imagination when a fit mythic embodiment is found for an archetype. Even Blake failed when he sought to invent live mythic beings; nobody dreams about Los, Albion, and the others. Greek myths seem to be inevitable in European fantasies. Even psychoanalysis draws on them. Not even

Christian poetry, based on angels and archangels and eventually reinforced with Celtic myths, was a sufficient and exhaustive alternative. Today a great poet, like Sylvia Plath, when faced with the old poetic problem of transforming the moon from a simple sign of its function into a symbol, solves it, and marvellously so, by calling Hecate back into service.

Compared with ancient times we are myth-starved, and Poe gave all the reasons why this should be so; poets with us have to labour at evocations before they feel that they can represent a convincing array of string-pullers behind the scenes, before they can readily, unconcernedly make raw facts mythically meaningful. We look determined when we have managed to master enough faith to make Dionysus work, as happens with Nietzsche and Pound, or when we get the Grail to work, as in *The Waste Land*. This is why we fail to appreciate the beautifully casual stories of gods in Homer, who could allow himself to sport playfully with them as with mighty personages so taken for granted that one does not need to be over-solemn about it, and even chaff and banter are allowed. Worship, it has been noticed, is rarely combined with respect. We fail to recognise the sublime insights of Homer's archetypal psychology because of his humour in describing archetypal personifications; yet there is nothing deeper than the idea that, behind cunning Odysseus as behind Hector lured to his death, the same archetype is at play, cool, crafty Athena; just as behind the dazed behaviour of pathetic, smooth-skinned Helen and soft, furtive, frivolous, lucky Paris there lurks impending Aphrodite, the Foamy-One. We fail to enjoy Homer's quarrels and threats among the archetypes because we mistake such familiarity for mockery, because his ready detection of archetypes is denied us who have to labour hard before we can even glimpse their majesty. Not so in the Greek world, in which when a man started kicking and foaming at the mouth it was not some term of the day's fashionable clinical jargon that came to the lips, but the name of a living being, Ares: the same god who made men battle-crazy was shaking the ill man's soul. When a child yelled in a nightmare one felt the presence of weird Hecate. The evocation of a live archetype is no less precise than the mention of a medical term, and it can certainly be more fruitful, as the inception of a psychotherapy. As for the poet who can mention archetypes by name, his task is enormously eased.

25 The inner triad

In poetry, of the two constituents of language, the referent and the vehicle, the former tends to specialise as purely inward and spiritual, pre-spatial time.

There is a supreme experience of inner transformation in which man's spirit, his witnessing selfless self, rises above the sentimental psyche and the bodily-conditioned instincts. This achievement is the greatest of goals, in the eyes of those who have attained to it, or at least approached it, or witnessed it in masters. It is also the arch-subject of traditional fables and of poetry. It borders on the inexpressible and calls for silence. Initiates are reticent about the rites and practices that lead to the goal, because the transformation they seek transcends the sphere of ordinary interests, be they personal or social. It stands above the merely ethical or exoterically religious level; so inevitably all that concerns it is best kept *sub rosa*.

Eloquent reticence is a definition of the poet's craft. There is an impressive tradition, comprising shamanic poetry from all over the world, in which the poet recounts his transformations from a bodily- or psychically-conditioned being to a free spirit, as Dante says, crowned and mitred above himself. The experience can be worked out in terms of a perilous voyage, a pilgrimage, a knightly quest, a war, a sacrifice and a resurrection, but the most frequent version is that of a courtship of the king's daughter. In Dante it is the love of the daughter 'of the King of the Universe'. The spiritual transformation is the work of this severe and merciful lady. She appears in the songs of Siberian shamans, in Chinese Taoist lyrics, in Hindu and Lamaistic songs to succouring Taras; in the Persian tradition she is the helping Virgin, in the Egyptian Isis; she becomes the untouchable lover that Bedouin lyrics transmit to Sufi poems and that these hand on to Provençal troubadours. Celtic and Germanic versions run parallel to the Persian. Dante and Petrarch carry on the tradition.

The poet feels his inner transformation with the fierce intensity of the pangs and swoons of love and, if an earthly love happens to fire his soul as well, he might splice the two, or see one in terms of the other. Whatever the biographical details, the poetic operation transforms into a love story a spiritual experience that must remain inexplicable to all those who have never disidentified themselves from their social roles and from their roaming thoughts; those whom Henry Vaughan's suggestion and warning have never reached:

> Leave, leave, thy gadding thoughts,
> Who pores
> And spies
> Still out of Doores
> descries
> Within them nought.

This process of self-transformation is explained by Donne in his *Ode: our Sense of Sinne*:

> But we know ourselves least; Mere outward shews
> Our mindes so store,
> That our soules, no more than oure eyes disclose
> But form and colour. Onely he who knowes himself knowes more.

The poet faces the task of leading us beyond the forms and colours known to the eyes and to the soul, into a spiritual reality, by making words resonate beyond their sound and meaning. He takes care of words and meanings, according to a Hindu simile, like a man trimming the wick of a lamp that lights up a scene. Only those whose eyes are not riveted to the finely trimmed wick will see the scene. That this is the secret both of Dante and of Shakespeare was proved by an American nineteenth-century essayist, Ethan Allen Hitchcock, who also preceded Jung's interpretation of alchemy. He simply took Dante as seriously as the man deserved. Dante wrote that Beatrice was the love of wisdom, the love that through wisdom produces contentment in one's destiny and contempt of the things that men usually allow to become their masters. How was such a love, such an attraction, to be represented otherwise than as the Pitying Lady, on whom all poets had hallucinated from the beginnings of time? Dante says: 'I contemplated her so eagerly, and with so intense a feeling of reality, that I could scarce withdraw my gaze from her.' His 'spirit of life' in his inmost heart trembled at the stronger god that had come to rule it; the spirit of his soul, to which the spirits of his senses carried their messages, started blissfully hallucinating on her; the 'natural spirit' in his belly started weeping, knowing that henceforth it would be ignored. A process not so very far from the awakening of Kundalini, which was followed by a new life and a divine comedy.

Shakespeare, Hitchcock proves, is as neatly explicit, though with him a boy takes the place of the Lady, and a dark lady that of the 'natural spirit'. Sonnet XIV offers the key:

> My spirit is thine, the better part of me.

Shakespeare insists that the two spirits or parts of himself in the Sonnet 'are one', with a disturbing dull part or character in between, the very same that, according to Hitchcock, appears as the wall separating Pyramus and Thisbe in the comic interlude of *A Midsummer-Night's Dream*. Things are made clear even from the point of view of sources in Sonnet CVI: writers of chivalry are to the Sonnets what the Old Testament is to the New. The avowed goal is, as with Dante, to acquire a god-like, crowned and mitred status (CXXI).

The revelation of this background usually meets with a hasty recoil. This revulsion has a function: it proves that the gist will remain unutterable; that only the trimming of the wick can be performed in the open, while the cloak of silence must cover the revelation for which the wick was trimmed.

The secret games of poetic personification take place as a rule in a psychic twilight about which poets prefer to keep silent. When they do speak out, a judicial deafness on the part of the reader makes up for it. On a few occasions, however, we are allowed to peer into the secret chamber; sometimes poets have been strangely induced to give up their customary reserve. On one such occasion,

Alvarez records that Sylvia Plath chose to disclose how she conceived the idea of one of her poems, about the archetype of Hecate.

'This poem, "Death & Co.", is about the double or schizophrenic nature of death – the marmoreal coldness of Blake's death mask, say, hand in glove with the fearful softness of worms, water, and other katabolists. I imagine these two aspects of death as two men, two business friends who have come to call.'

Another instance of rare poetic indiscretion about how an archetype acquires an image is contained in Keats's *Ode to Psyche.* A letter of his is preserved in which he states the metaphysical views that haunted him. His idea is that the Cosmic Intellect enkindles with sparks from its blaze the human minds, which are parts of itself, atoms of Cosmic Perception. They become personal identities only by combining with their allotted psyche and environment, whose painful vicinity schools them. The heart is the teat from which they suck their identity.

The scheme, says Keats, was parent to all Zoroastrian, Hindu, and Christian doctrines. He started turning it into a poem by letting it magnetise the mythic image of Psyche. He imagined her in the arms of Love, Universal Fire, as a girl embraced by a boy on a green meadow, and the feeling arose in him that an altar should be built in her honour. This might seem a far cry from the philosophic idea of the divine spark giving birth to personal identity. But the logic of symmetrical relations is at work, so if the spark suckles the soul, the soul shall suckle the spark, their mouths will suck one another; the youthful lovers are clasped in a warm embrace, and the poet who watches them, since he admires the girl, melts into her. This is translated on the conscious level in terms of religious devotion and the poet states that, since no pale-mouthed prophet is dreaming her dreams, he shall build her an altar and be her priest.

Keats is letting his imagination float adrift on the sea of images, but he is also philosophically alert and formulates the symbolic content in binary logic, so he does not confuse the symbol and its content, he does not place them in a relation of symmetry, as poets usually do, blending the thing and its metaphor. He persists all along in using contrastive logic, at the very climax of creativeness.

He allows us to pry into the dusky corner of the mind where ideas become images, like performers masking for the stage. We should expect, after his proclamation of intended priestly service to the divine girl – the soul – that he would proceed to describe the temple and the liturgy. This he does, but reminds us at every step, at every new image he introduces, that in the background there lies a corresponding invisible, inner, psychic reality. The kind of revelation Sylvia Plath entrusted to the letter, Keats here makes in a series of asides woven into the very texture of the poem.

He says that the temple to Psyche is built

> In some untrodden region of my mind.

The untrodden region is the unconscious, where opposites, pain and pleasure, are symmetrical:

> Where branch'd thoughts, new grown with pleasant pain,
> Instead of pines shall murmur in the wind.

The sanctuary shall be dressed

> With the wreathed trellises of a working brain,
> With beads and balls, and stars without a name,
> With all the gardener Fancy e'er could feign.

Fancy, in this case coincident with Coleridgean imagination, shall be placed at the service of the new cult – a worship of the soul in love with Universal Attraction. The brain will be its trellis: it will provide it with the sustaining latticework on which it may freely interlace its figures. The motif is of ancient standing: medieval Virgins sit beneath a trellis of roses and they represent Wisdom incarnate.

The notion of this cooperation of brain and phantasy is common in metaphysical traditions; sacred diagrams or mandalas are based on it. Mystics have always used imagination to obtain liberation; in this poem we are made to taste the very flavour, to feel the belly-deep urge that sustains such a creation of significant images. We are not simply informed about it in some scholastic phraseology, as in Keats's own letter about the general scheme of the poem. We are taken to visit the borderland where the seed, the primal vibration of the redemptive, liberating and image-forming experience, is felt, and where it is linked to images first of austere, towering, sombre pines around a small, rosy temple, and next of an arbour studded with flowers like a star-spangled sky; thanks to the slight intoxication of a scenery that shifts as a dream, we are introduced to the actual, living idea. Keats allows us to see a philosophical notion relate to the images that spring fresh out of the archetype common both to it and to them.

For once the enigmatic utterance of the possessed poet and the explanation of the priest-interpreter are enmeshed. The riddle and the answer are spliced. Yet even here the distance between the explanatory answer and the profundities of the riddle shall remain unbridgeable. In fact, they are underscored.

A poet reaches to the depths of being; he does not present us with a formula, but embroils us in a net of symmetrical relations, not for the mere pleasure that poetry can give but because no profound mind will ever believe that truth can be decently expressed in dry, dusty, ordinary language, however logical. With many this truism leads to scepticism. The Logos is despised. To the poet instead it means that, to express truth, all human and cosmic resources must be tapped, silence itself called in and listened to. One needs a total involvement, not only safely conscious but also riskily unconscious, not only rational but also bodily. This involvement must be based not only on contrastive but also on symmetrical logic, if the essential cosmic forces are to be brought to bear on the human idea, compensating for its imperfections, for its historical limitations, anticipating its implications, detecting its unavowed stirrings, uncovering its latencies, exposing it to the imponderable, adapting it to the total requirements not only of what the mind can check at the given moment but of what may emerge when we draw back into the regions where dreams form, through the land of sleep and rejuvenation, back to the fountainhead of absolute silence.

V *The Vision of the Rose*

26 The vision of the rose

Archetypes are imagining images, dreaming dreams.

When their connection to oneness is weakened and loosened, they collide with one another and common dreams and disordered fancies result.

When instead they draw to oneness, they generate intellectually inspired and life-enhancing visions. All the archetypes then converge to Oneness so that shapes and colours are foreshortened, and their true, relative dimensions appear. Converging archetypes are like petals spreading out of the bud and heart of a rose.

The most typical visionary scene is that of the animated, breathing rose – or, in the East, a lotus.

He who knows metaphysical experience is above all names and shapes, even beyond visions; but around this supreme void, as a prelude to it or in its aftermath, the mind is visited by visions which through colour and form convey the peace and harmony of metaphysical experience.

Their colours and forms show unity in multiplicity. In them one may appreciate even and odd reconciled – 'with swift, slow; sweet, sour; adazzle, dim' – harmoniously apportioned out.

Such visions, ranging from that of a piece of chintz to cobwebs or to frost's winter traceries on window panes, were Jonathan Edwards's favourite illustrations of the scenario that can generate benevolence towards being in itself, as he termed metaphysical experience. Hopkins instead selected from the book of nature finches' wings, landscapes all plotted and pieced – and fell on the immemorial and especially Hindu incarnation of Allness, the brindled cow, which Nietzsche's Zarathustra also rediscovered.

These piebald, dappled, arresting scenes achieve unity in variety, and bestow peace mostly because they show the golden mean in action, being dividable by two in such a way that their smaller section stands to the larger one as the larger to the whole.

Apparitions and appreciations preceding and following metaphysical experience are not only identified by the 'divine' and 'golden' proportions of their design but tend to reevoke and retrace a small set of unifying motifs. Of these the vision of the rose or lotus is the main one; each of its petals is an archetype.

Other similar recurrent arch-symbols of archetypes convergent are a dazzling, swelling, swirling sea of light or fire, and the insphering of rotating wheels within wheels. Blake's traveller into eternity sees space all around him opening, funnelling into vortical shafts; he feels their pull and suck on all sides. But when they converge into one calm in-drawing pool of circling layers, metaphysical experience is nearing and soon the arch-symbol of unification in oneness shall re-form – the rose radiating from its heart and bud; the wheel with its spokes awhirl; the sea of light or of fire; the cloudscape flowering out from a central sun; the insphering of wheeling shapes round the sun; the hub of the living mandala. Into it one is drawn, swooning through soft folds of convergence: the symbolic scene comprises a winging through to the centre. Of this experience, the usual dreams of flying are but fragments and intimations. The assumption to heaven can be imaged in the shape of an advancing prow or of a flying chariot or of a mounting steed – 'as penetrating as light' runs the Sanskrit stock epithet.

'Soaring into the sun's glory' is a stock simile of metaphysical experience, of unity with Brahmâ or Savitri in Hinduism and with Sambhogakaya in Buddhism; Dante's final metaphor is a flight into the source of all light, into the heart of the Rose, which mirrors the experiencer's face.

> Nimble rapture starts to Heaven and brings
> Enthusiasticke flames

says Crashaw in *To the Morning, Satisfaction for Sleepe.*

Sometimes the soaring flight of Parmenides and Plato's *Phaedrus*, of Cicero's *Dream of Scipio*, of Elijah's, Christ's, and Mary's Assumption, of Muhammad's ascent, as of all shamans before them, becomes a monkey-like sprightly climb up the sparkling cosmic Tree, each of its limbs an archetype – or up a notched pole, each notch an archetype again. Or up the cosmic Mountain, pyramid or Tower or menhir, with its progressive steps/archetypes, or its circling animals/archetypes. Dante combined the downward shaft, the upward-pointing mountain, the downward-growing tree, and the heavenly flight, the three in succession.

Jung noticed that when patients started healing they dreamt of mandalas, seals of Solomon, zodiacs, circles, wheels.

Traditional artifacts are all modelled on the dream-world pattern and so are solemn social arrangements.

The one and supreme monarch sits enthroned in the central, final hall, where all courts, archways, galleries lead. In the royal park, the first zoo, all animals are gathered, as on the slopes of the sacred mountain (at the various stages of his ascent to heaven the shaman sees archetypal fish and winged archetypal quadrupeds flying). The royal park includes, as Eden did, 'trees of all kinds', the whole set of archetypes in vegetable language. At the royal court whoever typifies an archetype must show up.

Antimonarchist feelings are not enough to escape the constraints of symbology.

Political unity, of whatever kind, always evokes the same stock images. Sovereign assemblies after the French Revolution fan out into an at least partial circle, comprising in each sector an archetypal colouring. At the hub of all sectors sits the ballot-box, the decisive here-and-now, where all colourings coalesce into the sheer light of revelation.

So the vision of the Rose develops into the total symbolical shape of political bodies, into the Tabernacle or the Heavenly City or the Garden. It also denotes plenitude in general in the round dances, the labyrinth dance, the morris dance and the sword dance, culminating in the 'rose' which is formed when swords point to the centre, waving, circling round it.

A poet haunted by metaphysical experience shall, like Eliot, insist on variations of the Rose, or, like Yeats, seize on all scenes in nature which appear patterned on the vision of concentrical, converging archetypes: flocks of wild swans noisily wheeling in vast broken rings over a lake; the falcon, upon a radiant sky, circling wider and wider above the falconer; flame-like figures perning in a gyre of molten gold.

Instead of a concentric pattern into which an image of the self soars and melts, the type of archetypes converging can be a spiral unfolding from a zero-point corresponding to what was the Rose's bud and heart – a heart of sheer silence and darkness, a golden egg or embryo, in which a first throb resonates, then becomes a pulse, and finally a myriad pulsating rhythms which flash, sparkle, blaze into fireworks, dazzle, intoxicate, and subside again into silent darkness, revert to the womb, to zero-allness. The zero-point is represented sometimes as the coiled-up, egg-like, circular, winged sun-serpent, which turns into a cross, zigzags into a spiral, spins into an epicycle, curling up into a great matter-creating, creation-projecting whorl. The same pattern of volutes is drawn on the rice-floor in Malabar tribal snake-totem ceremonies of possession, or painted on rocks from Australia to East Africa. It shall meet the eye across the Atlantic, drawn on the floor of macumbas or of voodoo shrines with peculiar convolutions to denote the corresponding song, to symbolise the deity-archetype that is evoked, from whose angle Allness shall be sensed and brought down to possess the faithful during the ceremony.

The near-inexpressible zero-moment, the still unruptured cosmic egg, the still unravished and life-giving golden womb is symbolised in Kathakali dances by the prologue, which is danced and sung behind a curtain. The Kathakali curtain shows receding square figures which represent the waves of the deluge, symbolising the absence of forms, of *mâyâ*, of the principle of delusion. When the curtain lifts we see behind 'the painted veil', into the world of the dancing gods, of the revolving archetypes.

The same kind of curtain as is used for the prologue of Kathakali hangs in Malabar Orthodox churches, separating the apse from the nave. The nave is a ship, like a ship-shaped shuttle heading for the notch, for the entrance to supraformal reality, for the curtained apse where the unseen priest during the prologue to the Mass divides the Host, Allness and Oneness, into its archetypal parts.

The zero-point is also symbolised in the prologue to Javanese shadow-shows. A figure is planted in the centre of the screen – a leaf-shaped Tree of Life, which is also a life-wafting fan or a Gate of Heaven, a Two in One. It is next lifted up, and waved all over the screen, suggesting with its fluctuations and flutters the forthcoming plot in its supraformal, musical, wavy, snaky essence.

The zero-point is also represented by the tuning before a concert. When a musician has perfectly fixed the pitch, he has grasped the seed, the germ of the whole performance.

What the vision of the rose and its analogues are visually, the harmonics rippling out of a tuning-fork are acoustically. That jet of silvery notes is as enchanting as a breathing rose or lotus.

The first note is first repeated one octave above. Only the few who have an ear for pitch can perceive the difference between the note and its replica. Similarly only metaphysicians penetrate into the simultaneous oneness and distinction of the knower and the known. Only when the third note follows, at an interval of five tones from the second, does an ordinary ear notice simultaneous difference and harmony. Five and three, the archetypes now start to unfold in a suave relatedness to One.

Robert Browning dared talk of this visionary experience of the cosmos unfolding from silence into the archetypal tones, in *Abt Vogler*; the heart of wonder, he explained, is the 'third note' in which the 'finger of God' shows:

> Consider it well: each tone of our scale in itself is nought:
> It is everywhere in the world – loud, soft, and all is said:
> Give it to me to use! I mix it with two in my thought:
> And there! . . .

Such are the main images, the shapes attendant on metaphysical experience.

27 Comedy and wild dreams

When the archetypes are placed round metaphysical experience in due order, the mind first finds its orbit among them, and is finally fused with the centre.

Even when the psyche is unbalanced, while the lodestar remains visible redress is still possible.

When metaphysical experience is acknowledged as the centre of being, the various archetypes follow a natural gravitation towards their essence, and form a rosette. Just as iron filings gather round a lodestone into a rose of iron, or a constant whirlwind turns sand into a 'rose of the desert', so symbological instinct untiringly connects Perfection with the Rose, from India to Persia to the Medieval mystical rose of the divine hosts round the supreme Godhead, mirrored in the rosettes of cathedrals, in the ribs of their domes converging on the capstone. When instead the supreme goal of ecstasy and peace is denied, the result must be either the social zombie's utter insensitivity or the torments of the neurotic. When 'why do I live?' is suppressed, daily routine becomes nothing but the reiteration of the interrogative.

It is for the shaman, the bard, the priest or the sacred dancer unceasingly to veil and unveil metaphysical experience; while the clown in his ill-fitting, patched costume, with his dumscomb deliveries, doing everything backwards or upside-down, is telling the story of colliding or randomly related archetypes seen in distorted perspective, as reflections of matter and not vice versa. When everyday, socially or individually-conditioned reality is taken to be the true coign of vantage, the result can only be comical. The most holy rites of Dionysus, in *The Frogs* of Aristophanes, become variations on overeating and starving, pomposity and fear, lust and apathy, and the most solemn utterances turn to loose strings of clanging sounds. When common life believes itself to be self-sufficient and at the very source of truth, time and space are enough to give it the lie. Today's beliefs are the reversal of yesterday's, both are the laughing stock of tomorrow; what holds true with this tribe is anathema to the next. The rustic manners that are the staple of comedy are the type of all opinion unrelieved by meditation, of all custom unrelated to universality and eternity, of all assaults on custom lacking a metaphysical perspective.

The prancing, tumbling clown is the average man pursuing his daily goals and identifying with his social roles. When he knocks into walls, gets thrashings, chokes in mud, trips over stones, courts Dirty Bess, he suffers self-inflicted comical pain. He has no proper standards of measurement, lacks criteria of judgement. He only feels and acknowledges certain archetypes, out of relation with all the others, so they appear disfigured and out of proportion. He is consequently crooked, twisted round and bent over, hunched, crippled, limping.

Clowns give lessons in the infinite ambiguity of archetypes, which is lost sight of when a metaphysical perspective is lacking. Clowns associate opposites – manliness and effeminacy, humanity and beastliness, childishness and pomp, dexterity and blundering, boasts and avowals of misery. The clown is stern when joking and funny when earnest; in command he squeaks, in fear he brays. He insists on getting the social code all wrong. But the way he plays the game is precisely what it all looks like from above. In a self-centred and self-righteous society the complexity of archetypes is ignored, their dependence on metaphysical experience overlooked or denied.

Though with a touch of self-importance that a true jester should discard, Shakespeare's Jaques proclaims:

> Invest me in my motley; give me leave
> To speak my mind, and I will through and through
> Cleanse the foul body of th'infected world.

The fool dresses like a shaman from staff to bells, from coxcomb to motley. Very often he has one shoe on and one shoe off, like the mountebank among the eight Chinese immortals, Lan Chai-he, both man and woman, heavily clad in summer, dressed in cotton in mid-winter. The reason for all this in China is well preserved: once he and/or she rose to heaven on a cloud, leaving behind one shoe, the belt, the robe, and the castanets; he used to roam the streets deriding all common ways and ordinary pursuits. Another trickster to preserve the original significance of clowning is Yoruba Eshu, the Legba of voodoo, boy or old man in rags, whose function is to introduce the other gods, to set the scene for possession by the neglected, overlooked archetypes.

The high theological status of the trickster, just below the gods, finds its application in the observable fact that only a lively sense of the comical, a trickster quality, certifies that a person is actually, intimately, unconcernedly keyed up to the archetypal, divine level.

Comicalness is the hallmark of common dreams. Common dreamers fail to recognise this in their dreams. Certain mystical teachings insist on reversing the situation, on one becoming so naturally attuned to truth, that one is amused at comedy even in one's dreams. The ordinary man is divided against himself, his waking self is never free from the delusions to which his sleeping, deeper self is clinging. Liberation must take place also at the dreaming level, where shamming is much less easy. Otherwise in daylight self-deceit is nearly unavoidable.

The early morning of a liberated person should fit Shelley's description of how the Fair Lady awoke from her soul's nightly rambles:

> . . . her tremulous breath and her flushing face
> Told, whilst the morn kissed sleep from her eyes,
> That her dreams were less slumber than Paradise.

The proper significance and relatedness of archetypes shall not shine forth in the day if the nightly dream-world has been in havoc and shambles, a prey to nightmares, traversed by leering, roving inflicters of shame. All this must be purified by jest and gut-deep disidentification. The jester's staff is precisely Lord Shiva Bhairav's.

Only by unmasking and joking away the subtle, swift dream-creatures on the spur of the dreaming moment does it become easy, customary to dispel the delusions of daylight with a fillip; only by jesting in dreams can we truly assimilate the art of telling meanings from meaning-bearers, signs from referents, at a glance and with a smile.

What the jester shows up and displays upon the stage happens every night in raw, ordinary dreams, which reveal the absurdity that social conditioning, the rub and trial of broad day-light, deadens and smothers. A sorry psyche all out of tune dreams incoherent dreams and cannot laugh at them, while a liberated soul remains uninvolved, sees their comicalness and tends finally to dream only visions of bliss.

The world of imagination is bisected and symmetrical, so it will naturally tend to frame itself as the vision of the rose; but when archetypes cease to converge it disintegrates into ordinary, wild dreaming and inane phantasising. The world of imagination is therefore not neutral, its directions are meaningful. By the usual code, in guided daydream therapy, upward movements denote improvement and achievement and tend to unity; while downward movements imply dispersal, multiplicity. The past is felt to be to the right and the future to the left. So it makes sense to put to every image Hamlet's question to his father's ghost, whether it be a spirit of health or a goblin damned.

Control of dreams is the only sure way of checking and directing one's waking steps: the Western world pays for its belief in the supreme worth and status of the waking state by not knowing how to handle dreams, and the archetypes that dream dreams.

There is the opposite, famous case of the Senoi in Malaysia, who devote their best energies to the elevation of their dream-life. When flying in a dream, they are trained to wheel towards a revelation; when caught in dream-dalliance they are taught to enter into unrestrained bliss; when engaged in dream-battles, to achieve either victory or an understanding with the enemy. Thus they give to every situation the auspicious twist. They are ready for surprises; they know that dream-creatures are teasers, and capable of consummate treachery, that a dream-lover will pretend to turn into someone whom one is forbidden to touch. Do not fear to make a joke of it, the Senoi boy is told, and this supreme wisdom he shall carry over into his waking world.

Tibetan Buddhism teaches in its yoga of dreams how to stare down nightmares and bid dream-scenes change at will. As in waking yoga the body has to be worked on, one is supposed to work on one's dream-self during dreams, modifying one's size, turning oneself into a beast or a rock or a forest, and finally, having acquired the skill, into a Buddha.

One practises making the entire dream-scene multiply or shrivel up, till at the end the difference between dreaming and the waking exercises of the imagination becomes immaterial.

The peculiar light of the dream-world is especially meditated on, until the crude glare of day and the blind darkness of sleep are imagined and seen emanating from it and being reabsorbed back into it, unceasingly.

All the West has to show are a few hints by some mystics at the purification of dream-life. Active imagination was experimented with by Jung; and the psychiatrist Hanscarl Leuner has suggested that, after learning to handle daydreaming, one apply the acquired abilities to dream proper: a Saviour figure should be helped to emerge; threatening figures should be faced, dealt with kindly, offered food, but eventually also calmly, deliberately murdered. Special fluids should be created-imagined in dreams, such as spring water, or milk or urine, and sprinkled like holy water to cure all ills and dispel all evils. Finally Castaneda has introduced a consistent dream yoga to Western minds: start by looking at your hands while you dream.

28 Tragedy and sacrifice

The vision of the rose is structureless: it may evolve, spiral and spin, but it lacks plot, implies no struggle. It is a revelation of oneness, its substance is its essence, it is potentially what it actually is.

The wildest dream and the flimsiest comedy instead show a structure. It may not be precisely a narrative – which, according to Shaw, consists of a tenor pursuing a soprano with a baritone interfering, a twosome tending to oneness but having to take the triad into due account – but there must be a strict sequence of stages. Jung discovered its formula: there is a presentation ('I was in such and such a place'), a development, a climax, which is often a reversal, and finally an upshot or solution, which might be missed or suppressed.

This holds true of all dreams – even of the reversed kind that Florensky studied, which runs backwards, from upshot to presentation, but is subsequently remembered in the natural sequence. It may happen that there is a difficulty in breathing during sleep, this dream-symbology drastically images forth as death by suffocation, and immediately the whole set of events that might have preceded and finally occasioned death is flashed back, runs backwards from upshot to presentation. The sequel is remembered, however, as taking its normal time in a normal course of events culminating in death, their final cause. Dream-time can be elastic and reversible, like the time of antimatter. But, whatever way its actual time flows, even if it runs from upshot to presentation, the wildest dream has a structure, and expresses thereby man's need for meaning. It is this need which creates structures. These are subject to a concentric pull, inevitably tending to ever greater cohesion and compactness; but the loose texture of wild dreams and comedies is unstable, unsatisfactory. There is a need for more convincing, more closely argued and cogently articulate statements of meaning, for dreams less wild, comedies less laughable. As the gap between meaning and the limply hanging rigmaroles becomes wider, the latent need for significance grows stronger. So, however coarse and loose, all comic scenes, all aimless dreams, are virtual pleas for visionary experience. All structures are embryos of structureless meaningfulness.

But the distance between the two extremes – meaning at a minimum, as the bare structure of wild dreams and comedy, and meaningfulness at its maximum, as metaphysical experience – cannot be bridged without a mediator, a proportional mean, whereby wild dreams shall stand to the mediator as the latter stands to metaphysical experience.

Mankind has always sought the mean in tragic sacrifice.

Metaphysical experience is at the same distance from comedy as from tragedy, from wild dreams as from awed sacrifice. From a metaphysical, non-dual point of view tragedy is comical and comicalness tragic.

Between the two extremes of imagination, the vision of the rose and wild dreams, tragic sacrifice is the paradoxical linkage. The Greeks expressed this in terms that are still with us. The vision of the rose in Greek translation is Apollo, the Sun amidst the choir of the Muses. But, it was added, Apollo or Unity was, as Dionysus, multiplied, 'torn into winds, water, earth, stars, plants, animals', a dismemberment which dithyrambics, carnival, and comical revel routs (*kômê*, hence: comedy) intimate. Dionysus is the god of wine, the loosener, the dismembered and dismemberer. The haunter of vineyards, feeding on them, sacrificing them to itself, is the free, wild goat (*tragos*), the capricious (*caper*) zigzagging symbol of lightning – Dionysus in animal form. When revellers tore the goat to pieces and fed on its flesh, Dionysus was eating himself, sacrificing himself to himself out of love, out of cosmic completeness. The song (*odos*) that sang of this sacrifice was tragedy, the divine goat's song. Through the frenzy, the horror and the pity of tragedy, Dionysus became Apollo once more.

All this pantomime translates into symbolic gestures and tragic possession this syllogism: everyday, manifold reality denies the absolute, oneness, metaphysical experience; but the denial cannot be absolute. That which is by its own admission relative can only relatively negate; and that which relatively, partially negates the absolute, relatively, partially affirms it. The absolute cannot be absolutely denied, and is affirmed by the very cogency of its denial.

The syllogism comes alive, becomes a total experience, through the murder of the incarnation of the absolute. Only a divine victim will do.

The divine, the vision of the rose, and the comicalness of ordinary, deluded existence – are brought into tragic, shocking contact.

Aristotle thought that to produce the shock a tragedy must be 'put into sweetened language'. Ordinary murder then becomes a sacrifice, a making sacred of the victim, of the sacrificer and of the participants. Man is then 'purged of his inner passivity by virtue of an imitation of shockingly pitiful and frightful things'.

The precondition of the tragic effect is the existence of a deeply ingrained repulsion against the tragic sacrificial act, and only an identification with the victim can cause it.

The contradiction between love and murder triggers an implosion of the psychic world. The sweet language of love depicts the most absurdly comical event, wanton self-destruction. But a whiff from the rose mixes with the sickening reek of blood. The tragic depression of pity and horror levers up, reverses, the perspective of ordinary, comical reality.

In the Mass-like pattern of tragedy, the Father accepts – in atonement for the wild dreaming and for the comicalness of everyday life – the pity and horror of the onlooker, who sees Him sacrificing His own Voice, Himself, His own Son, in the wilderness of comical dreams. The onlooker may transpose: *he* is sacrificing his own comical self to a truer, selfless self; the two are one but have stressed twoness to purge their oneness of all trace of duality.

Tragedy can be patterned on a visit to the nether world. In this case, after a sacrifice, the archetypes in reverse are visited one by one, until at the end of the test reversal and apotheosis can take place.

The Mass and the Harrowing of Hell or Divine Comedy are the two prototypes. Their like is found all over the world from the Hainuwele cycle of the sacrificed Maiden of fruits and grains, to that peak of universal tragic tradition, the Balinese play from the Râmâyana about Shiva the Saviour, in which a young prince, the victim of his bewitched mother and of the equally bewitched prime minister, is bound to a tree, like Woden to the world-tree gallows, or Christ to the rood. On the prince, Shiva (liberation or metaphysical experience) confers immortality. This new quality shocks all the characters out of their spell. Evil Incarnate herself begs for liberation, and is mercifully struck out of existence. The comic characters in the play stress the tragic reversal: comedy is a mediator between tragedy and liberation as much as tragedy is a mediator between comedy and liberation.

Aristotle's classical Dyonisian tragedy, the Mass, and the Harrowing of Hell were all included in the coronation of Babylonian kings. The recital of the creation of the world introduced a last repast, with all the symbolism of food duly stressed, before the king underwent a series of humiliations. He was slapped in the face, boxed on the ears, obliged to bow down to earth. His tears were considered a sign of acceptance from above, the turning-point from comicalness to tragedy, after which he proceeded towards a pit symbolising death. There he sacrificed a bull, symbol of the sky and of light, and lit a bundle of bulrushes, symbol of unity and silence. He then died and became the planet Saturn, the distant Lord of peace.

The king's tearful mourning son reopens his father's mouth, takes his hand, resurrects him and triumphs over all foes. He ascends to heaven, to the bower of bliss, where a sacred marriage and transfiguration takes place.

The Osirian ordeal followed the same sequence, with the dismemberment of the saviour, the shedding of tears, the descent into the nether world, the mourning, the resurrection, the fighting, and the crowning glory, the marriage to Isis.

The insignia of final exaltation are the usual symbols that cluster round the Vision of the Rose – the horned or feathered luminous crown, a quartz crystal or golden throne, a cane or branch from a sacred tree. On the naked body a syndon is worn, a thread is tied round the waist, a cosmic mantle or shamanic robe thrust over the shoulders – even today at English coronations.

The patterns of tragedy and sacrifice are those of initiation, which is always death and rebirth. The possible ordeals comprise all that the suffering hero might endure: purging, vomiting, stripping, scouring, fasting, thirsting, waking, flogging, wounding. There is a procession or circumambulation of a sacred space, a fourfold crossing of the elements, a descent below earth, a bath, an exposure to air, a contact with fire. A formal instruction follows, a dance, possibly a possession and/or an hallucination induced by smoking or breathing incense, by looking at a flame and at a design, by being sprinkled with water, by hearing or reciting litanies, by eating the flesh and drinking the blood of a victim. At the end the new initiate is enthroned and crowned.

A tragic, initiatory pattern of interpretation, applied to life's reverses will help hallucinate out of them. In Christendom one identified with suffering Jesus – or with labouring Hercules if attracted to heathen antiquity; with dying Ali and his family in Shiah Islam; with Rama and Sita in India. All religions provide such a means of magnifying away one's ordeals.

But there remains the danger of inflating the ego. Sometimes the cream is skimmed off the seething ego by the institution that runs the myth and incidentally makes the payment of tithes the precondition to legally valid tragic identifications.

The honest-to-metaphysics method should instead insert comedy in the initiatory tragedy. Trickster figures, fools in Shakespeare, the joking at initiations, the lewd banter at weeping Demeter out of her mind with grief at Eleusis, all ensure that the identification with the suffering Hero becomes, instead of a stumbling-block, a stepping-stone towards metaphysical experience.

Never lose sight of the trickster! He guarantees that the sign is not taken for the referent – which is the one basic mistake man never fails to make. And yet no greater blunder exists. With a trickster present, stuffiness cannot stifle life. This should not be mistaken for a watering down of tragedy, or for the tame reassurance of 'There is no absolute evil. There can be no radical tragedy', for the shallow psychic hygienics of mild humour.

The true way is that of an intensification, a purification both of the tragic and of the comic spirit, which must be separately distilled out of the mixed, grey broth of everyday life, and then brought in contact with one another: Christ eking out his life amid the carnival mockery of the soldiery. It is the dissonance that is liberating.

Tragedy should be interspersed with comedy, but its sweet voice must outweigh the harshness, power and spell of comicality so that its structure, its inherent urge for meaning, comes to the fore in a crescendo, with the energy of an ascending helix: from the presentation, which is a challenge and a conflict – the Greek *agon* – culminating in a death or dismemberment (*sparagmos*) implying adoration and *pathos*, to the mourning or deposition or descent into the nether world, which is finally reversed, metamorphosed into a resurrection or elevation – the Greek *anagnorisis*.

Single aspects can become independent, such as the reversal or metamorphosis of the climax in the cycles of Puss-in-boots, of the loathsome-hag-into-beautiful-bride, of the toad kissed into Prince Charming, or of Beauty and the Beast. The presentation can appear self-sufficient in taunt songs, duels, epics or exorcisms. The gist of tragedy and of all ritual offerings should be the sacrifice of selfhood, of the magnetisms that hold one's usual self together. The offering up of the gross and subtle body to the Witness effects the tragic and glorious reversal, with the realisation that the sacrificed wills his sacrifice, if he is beyond duality – beyond the slayer and the slain.

The final vision of the rose is sometimes marked by a passage to the majestic, triumphal (*tri*umph means a three-foot beat) anapest ∪∪-, after the hopping iambics ∪-, ∪- of comedy and the solemn trochees and sweet dactyls of tragedy -∪, -∪∪.

Tragedy follows the scheme of the lullaby. Its finale corresponds with the normal trochaic heartbeat.

A tragic access to the triumphal, final Rose of Archetypes is the purpose of rosaries and bead-necklaces, in which each archetype is focused in succession, as all animals are imitated one after the other during the preparatory session of the shaman, as all directions are meditated on in sacred circumambulations. The glorious vision also inspires the creation of praying mills, prayer wheels, divining wheels such as the roulette of Delphi; and above all the round dances centred on a pole, a pit, a stone, an altar, a victim wriggling, a person possessed, or, better still, a performing shaman, alone or with his helpers. The centre is the source of vision. Alas, the centre is less often a pirouetting dancer than a precious, tragic gush of blood, more intoxicating than wine. The sight of tortured innocence shatters the onlooker's soul, sick with qualm, love, and outrage, excited beyond them and finally emptied, serene. Man has always insisted on his horrified and horrible identification with an animal victim. Sometimes the identification takes a heinous form; the sensitive empathy with life's delicate traceries is brutally numbed, and dubbed squeamishness. Truly satanic is the cold rapture, the thrill at feeling oneself hovering as sheer, deliberate will-to-power above the throes of one's own psyche, which clings, with desperate love, to the gory struggling victim. One can be murderously ravished. There is a strange, complex thirst for life-blood, a soul-sucking love; bodies are murdered to obtain their psyche; at public executions in England women were observed endeavouring to be stroked by the still-quivering hands of the hanged. Perhaps something of the kind is at work in all beasts of prey, whose voices are identical with those of their victims; it is as though a bond of sympathy tuned the sparrow-hawk's voice to that of rabbits or kittens, and modulated the howl of the wolf to a sinister imitation of a bleating lamb, or of a roaring bull, as Chateaubriand observed.

Shamans in Siberia dart off into the invisible world as soon as the horse has been slaughtered, to secure its soul and ride it to the very sources of being. Bororos dance in the skin of the sacrificed jaguar until possessed by its soul, while their womenfolk bewail the animal's death.

Steaming blood is supposed to confer possession. Blood seems to help into a trance and out of it, especially causing or dispelling possessions by the spirit, the archetype of the victim. All ingredients of religious ceremonies – magnetised water, incense, fire, chanting and blood or wine – had the practical object of helping in and out of an archetype. Can there be a knowledge and a cleansing that is not effected by sickly blood or by a reminder of it? Without a whiff of brimstone, is purification possible? Porphyry, the sublime Platonist, asserted that bloody sacrifices were degenerations from primal innocence. At the centre of the ring there has not been always, necessarily, tragic sacrifice – but only the Vision, only a drumming shaman. In Siberian versions his voice soars skywards, while he stoops forward, shuffling with a slow left foot and a swift right foot, then leaping and howling himself into ecstasy.

The chorus of onlookers circle, gripping scarves, or with linked hands, or with hooked elbows, shuffling, answering, echoing, adding momentum to the spin, till they are swept off their feet, drawn up into the whirlwind of the Spirit. Sometimes there are many circles, which can stand for the various archetypes; they proceed in opposite directions, with rhythms and speed in counterpoint. The Yuroks of California know how to stage up to ten concentric rings. The Far Oer and Finnish *Sigurdsvaket*, Siegfried's wake, is a round dance centring on a soloist, in which Siegfried's tragedy is responsorially chanted.

The tragic meandering, labyrinthine dances, the imitations of mating or warlike clashes, and processionals, curling, waving serpentines, all end in the glory of Ring-a-ring-o'-roses.

29 Centres of transformation and healing

The first aim of spiritual education is to reach the vision of the rose. A Wiradjuri Australian tells the story of how his father took him out into the bush when he was a boy: 'He placed two large quartz crystals against my breast, and they vanished into me . . . like warmth. This was to make me clever. He also gave me things like quartz crystals in water. They looked like rice and the water tasted sweet. After that I used to see things my mother could not see.' Nor has the father finished with him yet. One day he helps him soar to high heaven, there to behold God, and the enormous quartz crystals extending out of God's shoulders, like transparent, glistening petals.

How did the father manage it? We are informed that he gave his son sweet-tasting water to drink.

Water is often changed, charged, to help hallucinate. Instead of the Wiradjuri crystals, saffron and camphor are dissolved in Hindu holy water. In Bali, apart from chanting mantrams over it, a blossom is sometimes dipped into it. The faithful drink it or are sprinkled with it, and hallucinate, receive the visit of a god, eventually even become for a while the god, the archetype itself. What is more, it is water again that helps them hallucinate back to normal. This is important, because visionary experience and trance are the first but not the final goal. What matters is the capacity both to enter and to leave such states, the ease with which one learns to swing in and out of them. Buddhists warn that attachments can be formed to the world of gods – the entranced, the joyful and powerful and healing gods – attachments which become hindrances. Nostalgia for Edens can be a harmful, weakening form of mental indulgence. Vision and rapture should matter less than disidentification and enduring liberation.

But they certainly matter more than anything the world has to offer. So it is small wonder that localities like the spot in the Wiradjuri bush become in time the sites for holy shrines. Especially if singled out by a special stone, and if a source of peculiar water flows nearby, with a lulling, soothing murmur – somewhere to come to dream healing dreams.

In time a ritual develops, a building rises on a lay-out that reproduces the vision of the rose.

The best that man has ever created has been lavished through the ages on such centres of healing and of renewal, in return for the joys they have offered. Life is a dull affair when they disappear or become lifeless. Without them art dies out, and manners become brutal; the taskmaster takes over from the priestly mesmeriser. This happened when men convinced themselves that Wiradjuri-like bush education must be superseded, that things were no longer to be set to order by adjusting their archetypal pitch, by having visions. Under the new dispensation tangible changes, which are now considered the only worthwhile achievements, must be effected solely by tangible means. On this article of faith, as Simone Weil explosively observed, all of modern science hangs or falls. Everything in nature is obliged to conform to the paradigm of unskilled manual labour. The universe is reduced to nothing but measurements of energy spent and retrieved, to the exclusion of all other models – finality, wholeness, harmony, archetypes. They are dubbed unscientific. Till, at last, they are the only dirty words left.

So now healing, transformation, holy dreaming centres have disappeared. One roams the world no longer as a pilgrim, hieing from shrine to shrine, but like a dog sniffing out old bones. Anubis-like, mercurial travellers only find a semblance of skill at holy dreaming at the church on the Greek island of Tinos, or in Nakshbandî Sufi centres in Afghanistan, where over the sleepers healing gestures are made and holy formulas recited. A semblance of the Wiradjuri insertions of crystals into the body is what can be seen among Philipino or Brazilian spirit-surgeons, who, like Araucanian, Dayak, and Siberian shaman-surgeons, seem to open up and operate ailing bodies. Loss of blood is conspicuous where the patient's acquiescence is least. All is performed on the strength of the shoddiest of archetypal systems. So one seeks out the adepts of the Chinese Man Sun Society near Perak in Malaya, whose method is better known and apparently not so shabby. They live sequestered in caverns for a period, gathering sacred objects, those that destiny singles out through sudden revelations as living symbols of the quest. They compose a reliquary or medicine pouch. To these holies prayers are daily made; in the body and in the psyche certain states are conditioned to the thought of them. The adepts train themselves to trance at will. While they open up to possession by the founders of their society, aides must stand by burning paper dolls of other, undesired subtle presences that might wriggle into the trancer. Before performing surgery, the adepts check their transformation. A sensation of heat must proceed from the belly to the brain, which seems to burst, till finally the whole body is aglow. Swords are thrust through it, and it remains unharmed. The arms are plunged into boiling oil, and emerge unscathed. This is nothing so very exceptional for Chinese spirit cults. Maniacal states, after all, make for anaesthesia – and a modest manipulation of internal sensations of warmth is even practised in common Western autogenic training.

A Man Sun surgeon is turned into a whirling flame; his forceful emanations seep into the inmost soul of the patient stretched out, offered up to the powerful archetype of Sacrifice. Their two souls coalesce; the patient's body accepts the change of destiny.

Our pilgrimage should move on, after Perak, to a Mediterranean township, Galatina, near Taranto, the land of tarantulas, so awe-inspiring to Tarentinians that they became to them the prime signifiers of archetypes, goddesses like the Hindu and Far-Eastern Taras.

Tarantulas build their webs cosmogonically and triadically. First phase: they thrust themselves down head-first, and hang dangling from their thread; in the rituals of many peoples initiates are thrown off a cliff with a foot secured to a long cable – to get the feel, as in sudden death, of an instant unreeling of all their life-story. Second phase: the tarantula extends its thread in all directions; from the centre to which it has let itself drop, it now radiates star-like, spins out its threads – like spokes issuing from a hub. Third phase: from the web's centre the tarantula spirals out radially, linking the rays of the star, like a basket-maker, in widening circles. The same triadic scansion obtains in the sword dance and in morrises, from Scotland to Spain. How can a sensible heart fail to adore a tarantula? Each kind of tarantula, fiddlers discover, responds to a kind of tarantelle, to a certain rhythmic pattern – to an archetype. So when people around Taranto were seized by panic, or by depression, or felt obsessed, they knew they had been bitten by a tarantula. They had to come to terms with her, which meant becoming her, to the very extent that they had unknowingly dared to ignore her and provoke her attack.

So one day, at the feast of the tarantulas at Galatina, I approached some old women and put them the question: 'How many tarantulas are there?' They racked their withered old brains, consulted among themselves. When they were small children all this was already on the wane. A few slender shreds of wisdom emerged: 'There is *La Muta*, the Dumb-one, she pricks you and you turn mute as a stone. There is *Esterina*, so shrill, such a coquette. There's *Pupetta*, Dolly; when she gets hold of you, you become as silly as a child.' A Hindu or Tibetan would comment: 'Of Taras there are as many as your soul may need.'

Once a year women who have been bitten by a tarantula are brought to Galatina. It is the feast of St Peter and St Paul. The cathedral of Galatina is dedicated to St Peter, and in it a holy stone (*petra*) is worshipped – the first identification sign of shrines. Just across the road stands the chapel of St Paul, with a well of holy water – the second identification sign of shrines.

Paul and Peter replaced the holy twins, Castor and Pollux. Castor the nightly one was a tamer of horses; he dealt with natural forces, archetypes. Pollux, the late Pythagorean Lydus disclosed, was the Monad, above Nature – Oneness at peace, compact as a stone. Pollux is Apollo-, and Castor Dionysus-like. St Paul was a leader, a tamer of congregations of god-possessed females speaking in tongues – a Dionysus. In this square where the very model of Dionysian tambourines seen on ancient vases are still peddled at feasts in plastic versions, St Paul's full name is 'St Paul of the tarantulas'.

Sobbing families carry to St Paul's chapel, to the holy well, the victims of the tarantulas. Their swoon is visibly painful. They sit with closed or haggard, staring eyes on the benches along the walls of the small, stifling chapel, where the fiddlers also gather. Relatives stand guard all around; the sighing woman is stroked and consoled. A tall taper is lit and held in front of her, as in front of a corpse or before an altar. All of a sudden she starts panting and screeches out a blood-curdling 'Eeh, eeh, eeee'. It chills the spine. When it starts, the amused onlookers outside the chapel move away; you see their sniggers become embarrassed and pained. Now the chief fiddler moves up to the woman, he dangles before her glassy eyes ribbons of various colours. One she snatches – the colour of her tarantula. The shaman's coloured ribbon symbolised the rainbow, the bridge to heaven. The ribbon hanging from the wheel on top of maypoles represented the rays of the circling sun – like the crystals from the shoulders of the Wiradjuri Godhead. Colours are like archetypes, refractions of the One light. The colour of the ribbon the woman selects gives the cue to the music.

The fiddlers hint at this or that tarantelle until to one the woman's legs frantically react, whirling her into an irrepressible dance, twisting and turning her round. Hoarsely shouting she leaps on the altar; from there she jumps onto the high, narrow cornice, circling round it like a trained acrobat, flying, waving her ribbon.

When the archetype has had its way, and spun its vortex, the woman collapses, exhausted, bathed in sweat, at peace. Now she can be taken to the cathedral, and to St Peter's stone.

From Galatina the traveller in search of healing rituals turns to the Iranian desert. I happened there once to ask a Zoroastrian priest out of the blue: 'What do you do with your dreams?' 'We have ways of making use of them thanks to which there are no mentally deranged in our community,' answered his wife. And she disappeared to make a special tea, she said, of *ephedra*, leaving her husband to divulge the beautiful ritual.

When a faithful Zoroastrian feels off balance, he repairs, late in the evening, to the house of the priest, and is put to bed. The priest and his aides have prepared *ephedra* roots and set aside a bowl made of the seven metals, with its pestle. They sit round the bed.

The man falls asleep and the priest starts chanting the holy Book. Words poured into a sleeper's ear bear their messages deep down into him. In Yorubaland a father wishing to instruct his boy in secret lore whispers things to him in his sleep.

Zoroastrians wear a sacred cord round their waist. At prayer they undo it and do it up again. It is part of the shaman's apparel – ladder to heaven, lariat, climber's rope. In China it was also the string on which he flew the symbol of his detached soul, the kite. When the shaman is degraded to a juggler, the cord is part of his bag of tricks; with it he performs the rope trick and does his tight-rope walking. St Francis taught his followers to carry it round their waist, and use it as a scourge and as a rosary. Zoroastrians say that it symbolises the lower fields of energy and their tethering. It is made of twelve goat- or camel-hair threads in each of its six strands, which are reminders of the festivals in the round of the zodiac. In short, it is the vision of the rose, with all the archetypes gathered to it, embracing the heart.

During the long night ritual the officiating priest holds in his palm the sleeper's cord, linking it to his own.

At the same time his other hand is busy stirring with the pestle the *ephedra* brew in the bowl.

The priest's wife offered me *ephedra* tea to drink. 'You other people use it as a heart tonic. We gather it at a special date; we only use plants that grow up high in the mountains. It also gives a slight euphoria.'

At daybreak the priest sings the last hymns of the healing ritual. The brew is ready and it is poured out. Now the bowl is empty. It is made of the seven metals – like certain Tibetan bells whose harmonics thrill to the marrow. The pestle is rotated in it, and it starts ringing louder and louder. When the beautiful sound pierces the patient's sleep, the *ephedra* brew is poured suddenly down his throat.

The healing dream is nearly always that of the lovely heavenly bride Zoroastrians expect to meet after death. A loathsome hag to the wicked, she is the body of wisdom and bliss to believers; the very same maiden whom shamans met, who visited Taoist ecstatic poets, Sufis and troubadours, whom Dante called Beatrice and Petrarch Laura, the spirit-wife of voodoo.

To the traveller at the end of his tour it appears clear that the universe admits of a most simple arrangement, once one knows about metaphysical experience. When archetypes become separated from that experience of oneness, the world of chaotic, everyday dreams gathers like a mist. Between its comic delusions and metaphysical experience, only tragedy and sacrifice mediate. And between tragedy and metaphysical experience only the knowledge of the world's comic delusiveness mediates. Three main spheres exist: metaphysical experience and its reflection, the vision of the rose; the comedy of wild dreams; and the tragedy of sacrifice. They are like three linked circles and the central one is metaphysical experience.

Made in the USA
Monee, IL
26 July 2025

21944605R00085